The Mirror Book

The Mirror Book

Mirror Sailing from Start to Finish

PETER AITKEN AND TIM DAVISON

With Illustrations by Nikki Gately

John Wiley & Sons, Ltd

Other Wiley Editorial Offices

John Wiley & Sons Inc., 111 River Street, Hoboken, NJ 07030, USA

Jossey-Bass, 989 Market Street, San Francisco, CA 94103-1741, USA

Wiley-VCH Verlag GmbH, Boschstr. 12, D-69469 Weinheim, Germany

John Wiley & Sons Australia Ltd, 42 McDougall Street, Milton, Queensland 4064, Australia

John Wiley & Sons (Asia) Pte Ltd, 2 Clementi Loop #02-01, Jin Xing Distripark, Singapore 129809

John Wily & Sons Canada Ltd, 6045 Freemont Blvd. Mississauga, Ontario, L5R 4J3 Canada

Wiley also publishes its books in a variety of electronic formats. Some content that appears in print may not
be available in electronic books.

Anniversary Logo Design: Richard J. Pacifico

Library of Congress Cataloging-in-Publication Data

Aitken, Peter.
    The mirror book: mirror sailing from start to finish / Peter Aitken and
Tim Davison; illustrations by Nikki Gately.
        p. cm.
    Includes bibliographical references.
    ISBN 978-0-470-51938-7 (pbk.)
1. Sailing. 2. Mirrors (Sailboats) I. Davison, Tim. II.
Title. III. Title: Mirror sailing from start to finish.
    GV811.6.A58 2008
    797.124—dc22

                           2008001321

British Library Cataloguing in Publication Data

A catalogue record for this book is available from the British Library

ISBN 978-0-470-51938-7 (pb)

Typeset in 10/15pt Futura by Thomson Digital, Noida, India
Printed and bound in Singapore by Markono Print Media Pte Ltd

This book is printed on acid-free paper responsibly manufactured from sustainable forestry in which at least
two trees are planted for each one used for paper production.

Acknowledgements

The authors gratefully acknowledge the help of Shelley Baxter for typing the manuscript.

Some of this material originally appeared in Roy Partridge's excellent book, *Sailing the Mirror*.

The photos were taken by Liz Mansell, Andy Fitzgerald, Peter Aitken and Alistair MacKenzie. Thanks to Tom and James Lovesey for sailing, in the cold, in front of the camera.

Thanks also to Itchenor Sailing Club and Warsash Sailing Club for providing premises for the shoots.

Contents

Contents

1 Burgee
2 Gaff
3 Main halyard
4 Jib halyard strop
5 Jib halyard
6 Gaff jaws
7 Jib
8 Forestay
9 Hanks
10 Bow
11 Buoyancy tanks
12 Forward and
   aft mast steps
13 Jibsheet
14 Fairlead
15 Forward and aft
   shroud anchorages
16 Shroud
17 Kicking strap (vang)
18 Centreboard
19 Boom
20 Gooseneck
21 Mast
22 Thwart
23 Tiller extension
24 Tiller
25 Rudder
26 Mainsheet
27 Stern/transom
28 Mainsail
29 Batten/batten
   pocket
30 Luff rope
31 Downhaul

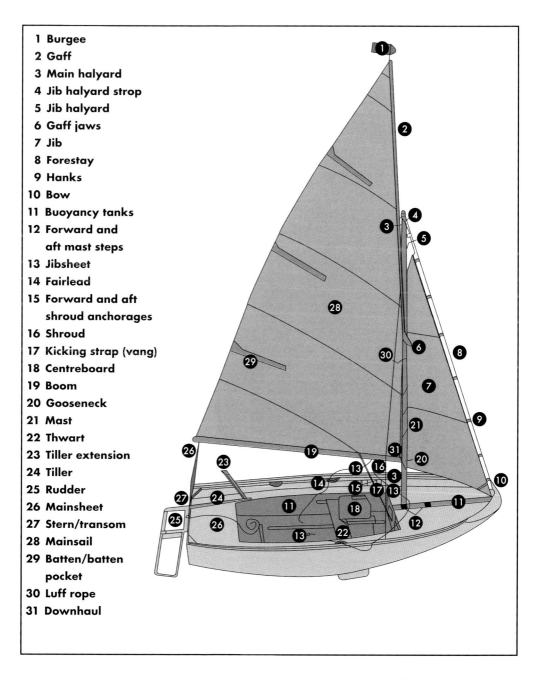

Sailing the boat

1 RIGGING A BASIC BOAT

The standard Mirror dinghy can be rigged in a few minutes – with a little practice! A sensible order for putting it together is given below. The boat should then look like the drawing on page ix.

- Point the boat into the wind.
- Loop the jib halyard strop over the top of the mast so the block hangs forward of the mast.
- Loop the two shrouds over the top of the mast (see photo page 4).
- Loop the forestay over the top of the mast.
- Attach the opposite ends of the shrouds to the aft (back) shroud anchorages.
- Run gaff and jib halyards through their respective blocks at the top of the mast, the gaff from stern to bow and the jib from bow to stern.
- Set the mast upright in the aft mast step.
- Fasten the forestay to the forestay chainplate.
- Loop the kicking strap (vang) over the boom.
- Fasten the mainsheet (the rope controlling the mainsail) on the port side of the transom. Lead the mainsheet through the eye of the boom and back through the eye on the starboard side of the transom. Tie a figure-of-eight knot in the end (see page 7).
- Attach the boom to the gooseneck.

- Slide the mainsail up the gaff and fasten the peak of the sail to the top of the gaff with a short length of rope.

- Insert the sail battens (thin end first) in their batten pockets.

- Fasten the clew of the mainsail to the end of the boom with a shackel. Tie a second piece through the clew and around the boom.

- Wind the luff rope around the mast. Tie a second piece through the tack and around the mast.

- Hoist the gaff tight to the mast.

- Secure the downhaul and luff rope.

- Attach the jib head to the halyard and raise the jib slightly.

- Attach the jib hanks to the forestay.

- Fasten the jib tack to the forestay anchorage with a length of rope.

- Fasten the jibsheets to the jib clew and lead back through the fairleads. Tie a figure-of-eight knot at the end of each jibsheet.

- Hoist the jib fully. Make sure the halyard is tight.

- Attach the rudder and tiller to the transom. Pull the rudder blade up and cleat the rope on the tiller.

- Check the bungs are all in place in the buoyancy compartments.

When afloat, put in the centreboard and push down the rudder blade.

2 RIGGING A GAFF-RIGGED RACING BOAT
Rigging the mast

First, put the strops on the shrouds, forestay and jib halyard over the top of the mast (photo 1). The jib halyard goes on first, followed by the forestay – on some boats these are combined. Then put on the shrouds. Make sure they are all at the correct angle – that is, they should be pointing at the chainplates when the mast is up. The mast may also have a crane for the spinnaker halyard. Spinnakers are covered in Part 2.

- Connect the shrouds to their respective chainplates (photo 2). This is usually via a pin and split-ring arrangement. Later, we will see how to use this to adjust the rake of the mast. For the time being, just make sure that the two shroud lengths are equal.

- Don't attach the bottom of the forestay at this stage.

- Check that the jib halyard and the main halyard are led through the pulleys correctly, from forward aft for the jib halyard and from aft forward for the main.

- Lay the mast along the boat, and push it aft (photo 3). This keeps the shrouds tight.

- Raise the mast, with its foot down into the front of the cockpit. Then lift the mast onto the mast step (photo 4). (If there are two steps, use the aft one.

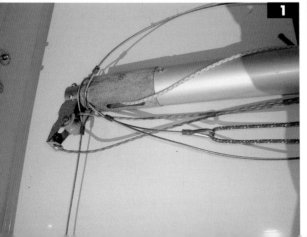
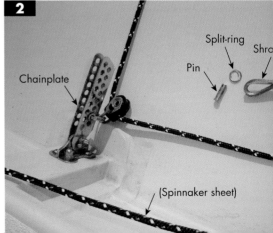

Chainplate

Split-ring

Pin

Shro

(Spinnaker sheet)

The forward one is for single-handed sailing, using a mainsail only.)

- Tie the forestay lanyard to the chainplate at the bow (photo 5). The trick is to bend the rope before you try threading it through the top hole of the chainplate. Tension the rope until you can twang the forestay to give a musical note.

- Check that the shrouds and halyards are properly aligned. Secure the halyards so they don't blow away.

Note that raising the mast is more easily achieved by one person than two.

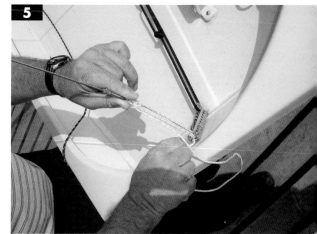

The boom

- The racing boom will probably come with the outhaul rigged (photo 6). If not, attach it (photos 7 and 8).

- Fit the kicking strap (vang) (photo 9).

- Fit the boom onto the gooseneck with the pin (photo 10).

- Rig the mainsheet (photo 11). There are two eyes on top of the transom. Tie the end of the mainsheet to the port eye, either with a bowline or simply by pushing the rope through from inboard to out, and putting a thumb knot in the end. (This helps the mainsheet fall into the boat rather than in the water.) Now feed the sheet through the pulley on the boom and then through the ratchet block on the other eye. Check that the ratchet block is the right way round – it should be easy to pull in but hold the sheet a bit when it is paid out.

6

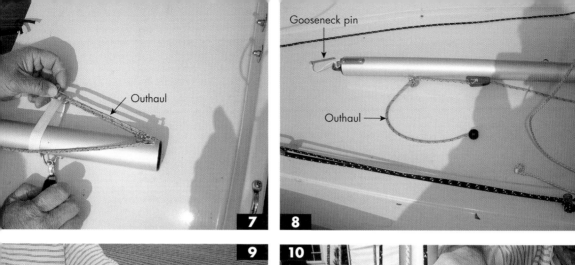

Outhaul

Gooseneck pin

Outhaul

7

8

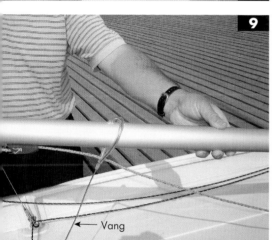

9

Vang

10

11

You're getting there! The next jobs are to attach the sails and then hoist them. The sequence is:

1. Hank on the jib

2. Attach the mainsail

3. Take the boat to the water

4. Hoist the mainsail

5. Hoist the jib.

Attaching the jib

- First, rig the jibsheet. Take the rope through the cringle in the sail and make the two parts of equal length. Then tie a thumb knot each side of the sail (photo 12). Alternatively, rig it as a continuous sheet.

- Attach the tack of the sail to the bow (photo 13). Hank the sail onto the forestay (photo 14). Note that the Mirror is unusual in that the jib doesn't have a luff wire, so the forestay takes the load.

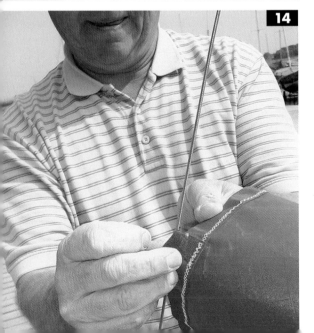

- Get the jib halyard ready. Look aloft to make sure it isn't twisted. Take the end of the halyard through the eye in the head of the jib, and also around the forestay (photo 15). Tie in a bowline. (This arrangement takes the strain off the top hank.)

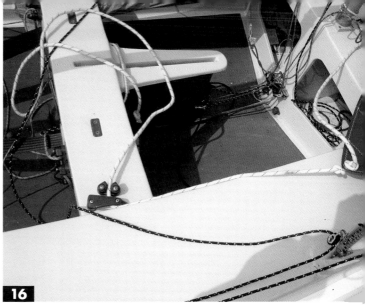

- Finally, lead each sheet inside the shroud and through the fairlead (photo 16). Tie a figure-of-eight in the end, leaving a tail so you can grab the end easily (photo 17).

Attaching the mainsail

- Most modern mainsails are kept rolled to avoid creases. Unroll it.

- The battens will usually be sewn in. If not, insert them at this stage (photo 18). Note I am holding a telltale.

- Check the lacing line – 1.8m (6 ft) – is attached to the top cringle.

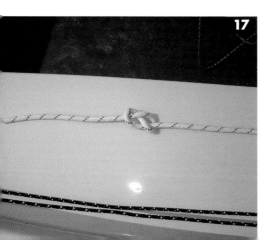

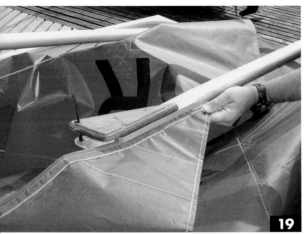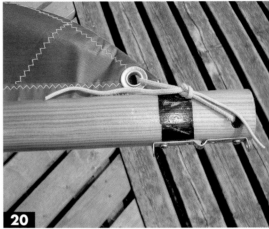

- Thread the main onto the gaff, from the bottom end of the gaff (photo 19). This is a two-man job. Tie the head of the sail so it aligns with the black band (photo 20). The sail is free at the jaws.

- Attach the halyard by passing it through the gaff band from top to bottom and tying a thumb knot (photo 21). This ensures the band can lie as close to the mast sheave as possible.

- Attach the clew of the main to the outhaul system (photo 22).

- Attach the jaws to the mast with elastic (photo 23).

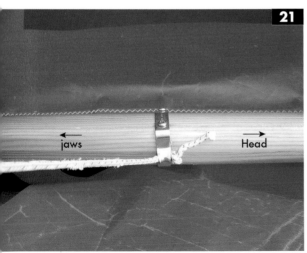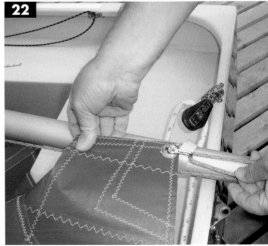

Doing a dummy hoist to get the lacing line organised

- Firstly, hoist the sail halfway. Thread the lacing line round the mast (inside everything) and through the first hole (photo 24). Hoist the gaff a little higher and repeat for the next hole, and so on (photo 25).

- After the last eye, take the rope round the mast, through the cringle again and tie off with two half hitches (photo 26). The lacing should not be too tight so that, later, you can pull down on the luff downhaul.

- Rig the downhaul (red string) (photo 27). (Most boats have a Cunningham to pull down the front edge of the sail but on a Mirror the cringle is in the corner of the sail so the control is called a downhaul.)

- When you have all the ropes perfectly positioned, mark them with a felt-tip pen.

- Finally, drop the mainsail – there is no need to undo the lacing.

Getting ready to hoist

- Attach the burgee (flag) to the top of the mast (photo 28).

- Attach the rudder, making sure the retaining clip is in place and the tiller is through the mainsheet properly. Swing the rudder blade up, ready for launching (photo 29).

- Put the daggerboard on the foredeck. Note the cut corner will go at the front – it is cut to allow the kicking strap (vang) to swing from side to side (photo 30).

When in place, the shock cord will go over the top of the daggerboard.

Advanced tip: The case is bigger than the board so it is possible to rake the **top** of the board back in light airs, and forward in strong winds. You can do this by making a suitable handle, and using more shock cord.

Take the boat down to the water and point the bow into the wind.

Hoisting

- Pull up the main first. Get it tight by 'sweating' the halyard, that is, pulling the rope sideways, then taking the slack through the cleat. The gaff band should be into the mast sheave (photo 31).

- The kicking strap (vang) is in place, but loose at this stage to de-power the sail.

- Set the outhaul so the gap between the foot of the main and the boom is about from your fingertips to your thumb – say around 12cm (5 in.) (photo 32).

- Then hoist the jib (photo 33). It should be fairly tight. Pull in the sheet and check there are no creases at right angles to the luff (front edge) – if there are, tighten the halyard a bit. But if there's a vertical crease along the luff, this 'knuckle' will stop you pointing – so slacken the halyard a little.

3 RIGGING A BERMUDIAN BOAT

Rigging the Bermudian boat is very similar to the gaff-rigged one:

- Attach the clew to the outhaul (photo 1).

- Unroll the mainsail (photo 2).

- Untwist the halyard (photo 3).

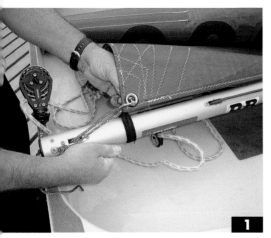

- Attach the halyard to the head of the sail, preferably with a ball arrangement (photos 4–7).

- Feed the head of the sail into the luff groove.

- Hoist, feeding the luff of the sail into the jaws of the luff groove (photo 8).

- Halfway up, put the boom onto the gooseneck (photo 9).

4

5

6

7

8

9

- Pull the sail right up. The tack (bottom, front corner) is loose at this stage.

- Attach the tack downhaul (photo 10).

- Hold the boat down. Sheet in the sail and check its shape (photo 11).

- Finally, pull up the jib.

4 SAILING THEORY

Take a careful look at the photograph on this page. You will see that:

- The helm sits on the windward side of the boat.

- The helm always holds the tiller in his aft (back) hand. He steers with the tiller.

- The helm always holds the mainsheet in his forward (front) hand. The mainsheet adjusts the angle of the mainsail to the centreline of the boat.

- The crew uses his weight to help the helm prevent the boat heeling. This means sitting to windward in strong winds, to leeward in light winds.

- The crew generally holds the jibsheet in his aft hand. The jibsheet controls the angle of the jib to the centreline of the boat.

- The jib and mainsail are roughly parallel.

How does a boat sail?

Wind is a boat's driving force. The wind flows over the windward side of each sail (causing pressure) and round the leeward side (causing suction). The resulting force on the sails is in the direction of arrows A and B in Figure 4.1, that is, it is at right angles to each sail.

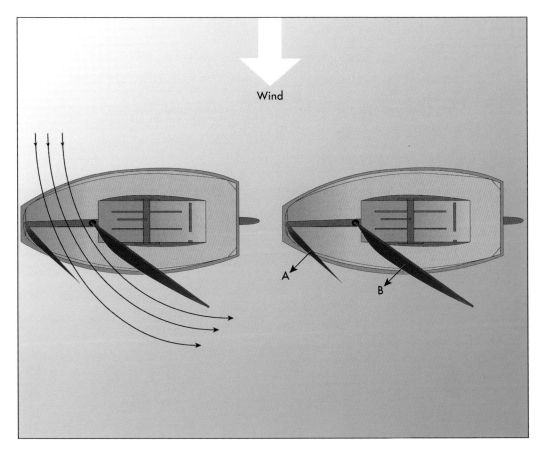

4.1 The wind force acts on the sails like this.

The force pushes the boat forwards and sideways. The forwards push propels the boat. The sideways push is counteracted by water pressure on the centreboard.

The helm's and crew's weight counteract the turning (capsizing) effect. The further you lean out, the more leverage you get – this is called 'sitting out' or 'hiking' (Figure 4.2).

If the sails are pulled in, forces A and B will be almost at right angles to the boat: the sideways force is maximum and the centreboard needs to be pushed right down to counteract it. If the sails are let out, the forces point forwards: there is no sideways force, so the centreboard can be pulled up (Figure 4.3).

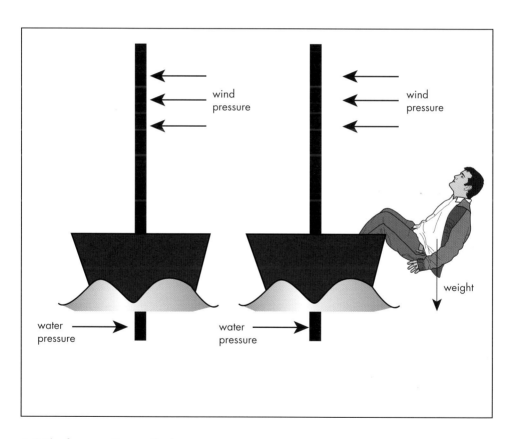

4.2 The forces acting on the boat.

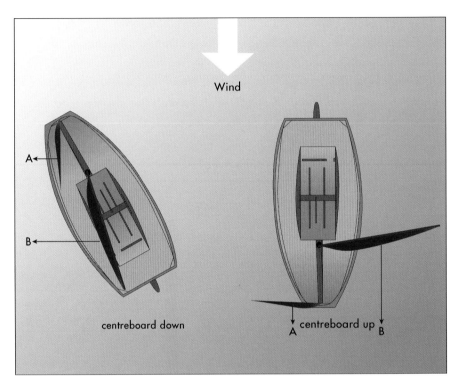

Wind

A◄

B◄

centreboard down

A   centreboard up   B

4.3 The sideways force is maximum when beating, zero when running.

How can I steer?

When a boat is sailing straight and upright the water flows past the rudder undisturbed. When the rudder is turned, the water is deflected. The water hitting the rudder pushes it, and the back of the boat, in direction C. The bow turns to the left (Figure 4.4).

In short, pulling the tiller towards you turns the bow away from you, and vice versa.

How can I stop?

It is the wind in the sails that makes a boat go forward. To stop, take the wind out of the sails either by letting out the sheets or by altering course towards the wind (Figure 4.5).

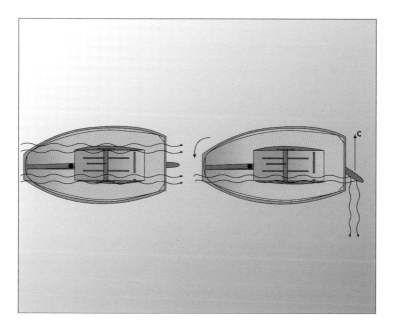

4.4 How the rudder works.

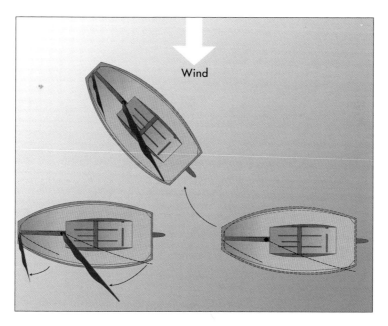

4.5 Two ways to slow down.

How can I tell which way the wind is blowing?

Everything in sailing is related to the wind direction. You can tell which way it's blowing by the feel of it on your face, by the wave direction or by using a burgee. Remember, the burgee points to where the wind is going.

Points of sailing

Look at Figure 4.6 below. There are three points of sailing:

1. Reaching – the boat sails across the wind.

2. Beating – the boat sails towards the wind.

3. Running – the boat sails with the wind behind.

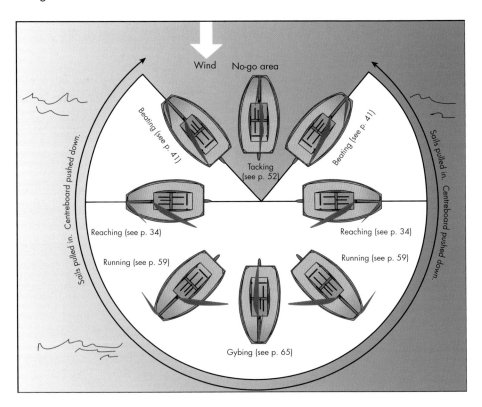

4.6 Points of sailing.

Reaching

The boat in photo 2 is reaching. It is sailing at right angles to the wind, which is blowing from behind the helmsman's back. The sails are about halfway out and the centreboard halfway up.

Beating

If you want to change course towards the wind, you must push the centreboard down and pull in the sails as you turn (photo 3). You can go on turning towards the wind until the sails are pulled right in. Then you are beating.

If you try to turn further towards the wind, you enter the 'no-go area'. The sails flap and the boat stops.

To get from A to B, the only way is to beat in a zigzag fashion (see Figure 4.7).

At the end of each 'zig' the boat turns through an angle of 90°. This is called a tack. The boat turns 'through' the wind – the sails blow across to the other side and the helmsman and crew must shift their weight across the boat to balance it.

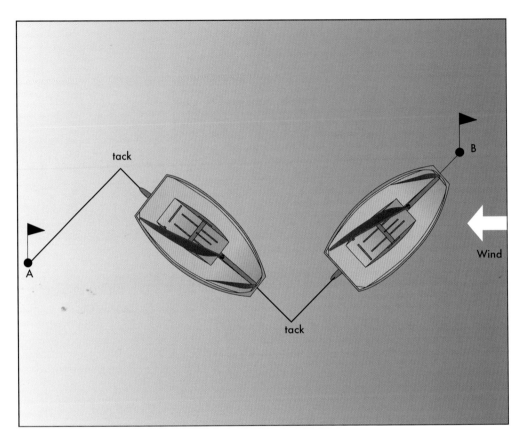

4.7 Beating.

Running

From a reach, you may want to change course away from the wind. Pull up the centreboard (not more than three-quarters up) and let out the sails as you turn. You can go on turning until the wind is coming from behind the boat. Then you are running (photo 4).

If you turn more, the boat will gybe. The wind blows from the other side of the mainsail, which flicks across to the other side of the boat. Push the centreboard down before the gybe, and shift your weight as the boom comes across.

5 A FIRST SAIL

Try to choose a day with a gentle breeze for your first sail. Wind is measured either on the Beaufort scale or in metres per second (see Table below). Force 4 or above would be unsuitable.

Wind Speed

Beaufort Number	Speed (knots)	Speed (metres per second)
0	1	0.5
1	1–3	0.6–1.9
2	4–6	2.0–3.5
3	7–10	3.6–5.9
4	11–16	6.0–9.4
5	17–21	9.5–12.4
6	22–27	12.5–15.9
7	28–33	16.0–19.5
8	34–40	19.6–23.5

A reservoir, river or estuary is a good place to learn to sail. If you are learning on the open sea, try to avoid an offshore wind (wind blowing from shore to sea) – you may get blown a long way from the shore. Always wear lifejackets, and stay with the boat whatever happens.

Rig the boat as described on pages 2 to 16, and launch as described on pages 29 to 33. As soon as you can, get sailing on a reach (see photo 1) with the wind blowing at right angles to the boat. The centreboard will be about half up and the sails about half out.

The helmsman sits on the side opposite the sails. Practise adjusting the mainsheet and steering. Try to get the 'feel' of the boat, in particular using your weight to balance the wind in the sails.

The crew sits wherever is best to stop the boat heeling. Practise adjusting the jib, which should be roughly parallel to the mainsail. Move your body to help the helmsman keep the boat level. (Reaching is discussed in more detail on pages 34–40).

Eventually you will need to tack (turn round – see photo 2) and reach back again. Tacking is discussed on pages 51 to 56. The crew needs to let out the jibsheet and pull in the opposite one as you tack. Try to tack smoothly, changing sides as you do so. If the boat stops during a tack, keep the tiller central and wait until the boat starts to drift backwards. Eventually it will turn to one side and you'll be able to get sailing again.

Reach back and forth until you have gained confidence. Try picking an object and sailing straight towards it, adjusting the sheets so the sails are as far out as possible without flapping. If a gust comes, let the sheets out. Try to keep the boat moving.

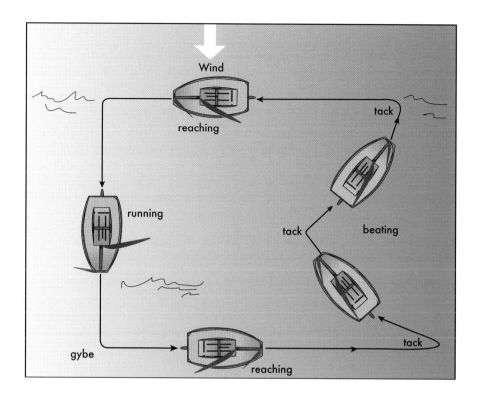

Next try picking objects slightly closer to or slightly further away from the wind. Try sailing towards them adjusting the sheets: the sheets should be pulled in more when sailing closer to the wind.

When you've had enough, head for the shore. If the wind is onshore, when you are about 50 m(165 ft) away, point the boat into the wind and let the mainsail down; then turn and drift ashore using the jib. If the wind is offshore, simply sail up to the shore letting the sheets out as you get near. Don't forget to pull up the rudder and centreboard in good time. Landing is discussed in more detail on pages 74–78.

The next steps

When you feel happy reaching and tacking, you are ready to try the other points of sailing (see page 22).

One good way to practise is to sail round a square 'course' (see above).

From your reach, gradually turn away from the wind, letting out the sails and pulling the centreboard three-quarters up. You are now running. After a while, push down the centreboard (to let the crew get across the boat), pull the tiller towards you and gybe. Now reach the other way, with the centreboard half down and the mainsheet half out. Next, push the centreboard right down and turn towards the wind, pulling in your sails. You are beating. Tack, and beat the other way. When you are far enough into the wind, turn off onto a reach, letting the sails out and pulling the centreboard half up. Try several laps.

Remember: The helm sits on the windward side. He keeps the mainsheet in his front hand, tiller in his back hand.

If you get out of control, let out both main and jibsheets – don't panic!

6 LAUNCHING

With practice, you will find you can get afloat quickly and easily in most conditions.

How you launch depends on the wind direction relative to the shore. However, a few points always apply:

- Rig the boat on the shore.

- Keep the boat pointing into the wind at all times. Let the sails flap freely – make sure the sheets are slack.

- The hull is easily damaged. Keep it off the ground at all costs.

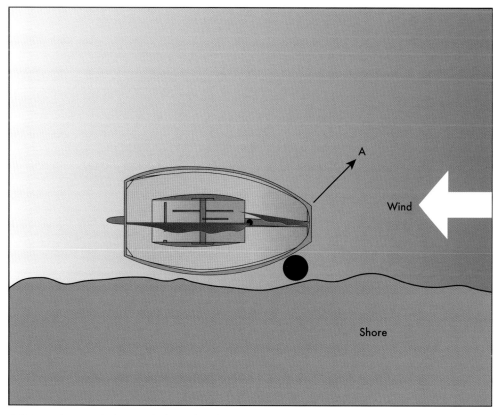

6.1 Launching with the wind along the shore.

Launching with the wind along the shore

This is the easiest wind direction to launch in.

1. Get your boat rigged, but leave your rudder blade up and don't put the centreboard in yet.

2. Put the boat in the water, keeping it pointing into the wind. The helm holds the boat, standing in the water near the bow.

3. See that your trolley is left safely – remember the tide!

4. The crew climbs aboard, puts in the centreboard and pushes down the rudder until they both just clear the bottom.

5. The helm makes sure that the mainsheet is running free and the tiller extension points towards him.

6. The helm turns the boat slightly away from the shore, pushes it forward and steps in on the windward side. Aim to sail in direction A. Pull in the sails, encouraging the boat to move forward slowly. Don't try to go too fast with the rudder blade up – you may snap it.

7. As soon as the water is deep enough, let out the sails (keeping the boat in direction A) and push the centreboard and rudder right down.

Launching with an offshore wind

Follow exactly the same method as for launching with the wind along the shore. DO NOT try to turn the boat round and sail straight out – it will sail away before you have time to jump in! Aim to get off in direction B.

Launching with an onshore wind

This is the most difficult wind direction for launching, because the wind tends to push you back on shore.

Put the boat in the water, following the first five steps described above. You will have to beat to get away from the shore, so choose which tack you are going to take. In the

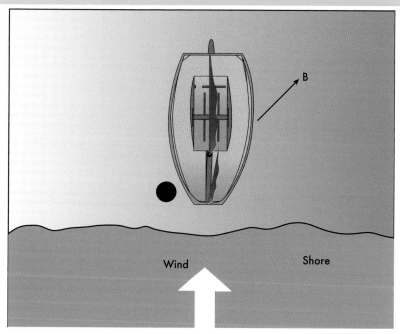

6.2 Launching in an offshore wind.

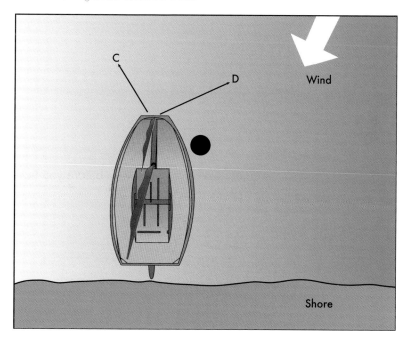

6.3 Launching with an onshore wind.

diagram, C is better than D because the wind is coming more from the right and C will take you offshore faster.

The helm gives the boat a good push and steps aboard. Pull in the sails quickly and hike out. Gradually push the centreboard down as you 'crab' offshore. Finally, when you're well out, stop and lower the rudder blade fully.

Launching in very shallow water

Wade out, towing the boat, until the water is at least up to your knees (deeper if the wind is onshore).

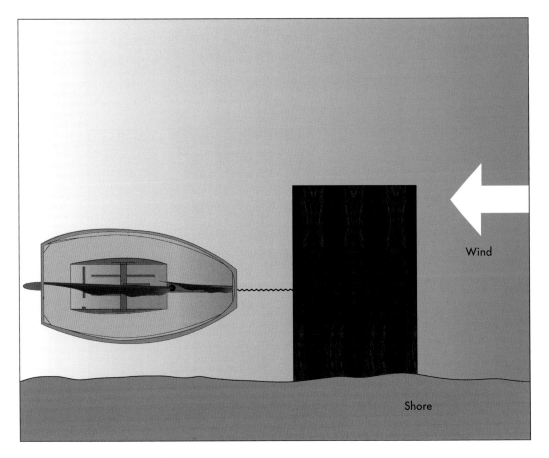

6.4 Launching to leeward of a jetty.

Launching in waves – onshore wind

Rig the boat at the water's edge with the bow into the wind. Decide which tack you're going on. The helm stands on the side that is to windward, with the tiller extension out to this side. The helm holds the mainsheet in his front hand while the crew stands on the opposite (leeward) side of the boat. Watch for a lull in the waves – it will come, but you may have to wait a few minutes. Run forward with the boat, and as the water gets deep push the boat forward. The crew rolls into the boat a second or two before the helm hauls himself on board. Hike out, and try to sail as fast as possible. If the boat gets washed back in, jump out to windward at the last moment. Try not to get between the boat and the shore – a big wave may push the boat into you and do you a lot of damage. If you do get trapped like this, keep your back to the boat or it may hit your knees 'wrong way on' and break your leg. But if it's that rough, maybe you should stay ashore!

Launching from a jetty

Be sure to launch your boat on the leeward side of the jetty! (See Figure 6.4)

To get aboard, pull the boat in until it is nearly sideways to the jetty, bow pointing to open water. The helm steps in onto the thwart, and pushes down the rudder blade and the centreboard. The crew meanwhile unties the painter and then steps aboard, giving the boat a push off. Pull in the jib and mainsheet and sail off.

7 REACHING

Reaching is fun! It's the fastest point of sailing and the easiest to control.

What is reaching?

The boats in the diagram are reaching. Their courses are roughly at right angles to the wind.

The secret of reaching is sail trim. Keeping a straight course, let the sails out until they begin to flap at the front (just behind the mast or forestay). Then pull in the sails until they just stop flapping.

The wind changes in direction every few seconds, so the sails must be trimmed constantly. Keep the sheets in your hands all the time, and 'play' them in and out.

If the sails flap, they're too far out. If the boat heels over and slows down, the sails are too far in. When the sails are about right, they will be roughly in line with the burgee and with each other.

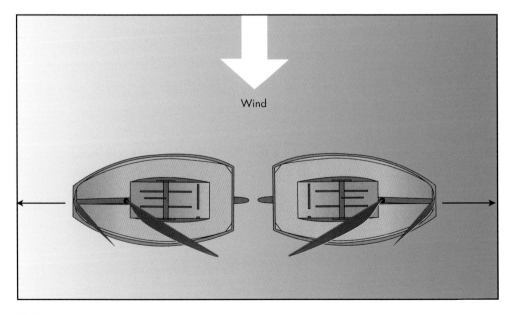

Wind

7.1 Reaching.

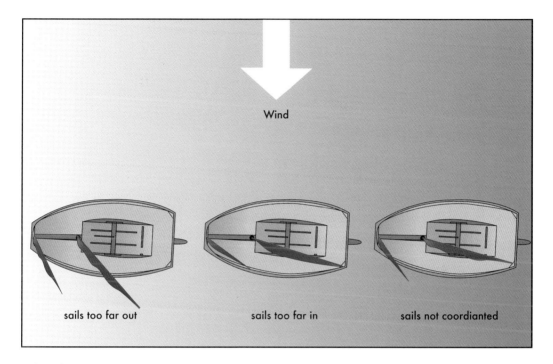

Wind

sails too far out   sails too far in   sails not coordianted

7.2 Sail trim.

Every time you change course, you must adjust the sheets – pull them in further if you change course closer to the wind, let them out if you change course away from the wind.

Steering

Try to keep a reasonably straight course: each time you alter course, you will have to adjust the sails. If there is a strong 'pull' on the tiller extension, it's usually because the boat is heeling over too much. Hike out to bring the boat level; the pull will disappear and you can steer easily. (In fact, you can steer by using heel.)

Trim

Both fore-and-aft and sideways movements of your bodies affect the boat's trim.

Normally, the helm and crew sit so that their centre of gravity (the midpoint of their combined weights) is on the centreline of the thwart. This presents the best hull shape to the water. Move forwards in light winds to reduce the amount of hull skin in the water

(and so reduce skin friction). Move aft in strong winds to lift the bow and help the boat to plane.

Move your weight to keep the boat absolutely upright. This will make steering much easier – if the boat heels, the asymmetric hull shape is forced to turn to one side.

Centreboard

Have the centreboard half up, to reduce drag and make the boat easier to handle. If it slips down, tighten the elastic shock cord. If you want to change course closer to the wind, push the centreboard down slightly; pull it up if you change course away from the wind.

Photo 1 shows good reaching technique. The helmsman and crew are using their weight to keep the boat absolutely level. The crew's attention is on the front part of the jib (as well as where they're going!) and he continually adjusts the jibsheet. The helmsman continually adjusts the mainsheet; because the boat is level, he can steer gently and easily. The kicking strap (vang) is tight, but the other controls are loose. The mainsail has a good curve in it for maximum power.

Gusts

Look over your shoulder occasionally to see if a gust is coming. The water looks dark as a gust travels over it.

When the gust hits, hike out further. If the boat still heels over, ease the sheets out until the boat comes level. Don't forget to pull the sheets back in again as the gust passes, or the boat will heel over on top of you (to windward).

Don't let the gust turn the boat round into the wind. Be decisive with the tiller and keep the boat going in the direction you want.

Sail controls

The mainsail should be set so there is a good curve in the sail.

The kicking strap (vang) should be on its 'normal' setting. 'Normal' is defined like thin. On a beat, pull in the mainsheet until the leeward section (at the stern) is vertical. Now pull on the kicking strap (vang) until it takes up the tension. Then pull more until the top block moves 25mm. This is the 'normal' setting for the kicker, which you can use as a reference for beating, reaching and running.

The downhaul should be loose. Let the rope off until creases appear along the front edge of the sail. Then pull in the downhaul until the creases just disappear. The maximum belly should come forward to the middle of the sail.

The mainsail outhaul should be loose. You should be able to get your fist between the foot of the sail and the middle of the boom.

In stronger winds, all three sail controls should be tighter. In light winds, they should be looser.

Going faster

If you want to win races, it's essential to be able to reach fast. Here are some points to watch and ideas to try:

- Keep the boat absolutely upright.

- Adjust the sheets all the time.

- Use your body weight. Hike out as far as you can. Move back in gusts, forward in lulls. If the boat heels, try to bring it upright with your weight before earing out the sheets. Don't just set there like a lemon!

- Steer a straight course. Don't weave about – the rudder acts as a brake each time you use it.

- In a strong gust, alter course away from the wind, easing the sheets. Get back on course when the gust has passed.

- Turn away from the wind each time a wave picks up the boat. Try to surf on each wave.

- Try fixing a 'telltale' on your jib about 60cm (24 in.) up from the foot and about 15cm (6 in.) back from the forestay. When the sail is properly adjusted, the wool should stream back on both sides of the sail. If the jib is too far in, the leeward telltale will collapse; too far out, and the windward one will collapse.

- Use the spinnaker whenever possible (the spinnaker is discussed in Part 2.

Reaching in light winds

Reaching in light winds needs patience. Try to keep still – if the boat rocks about the wind is 'shaken' out of the sails.

Steering

Hold the tiller extension gently and try to alter course as little as possible. If the boat is stopped, try using your weight to bring the boat gently upright, at the same time slowly pulling in the mainsheet – but only once if you're racing!

Trim

Sit right forward to lift the stern of the boat clear of the water. This cuts down the wetted area of the hull and hence the friction between the hull and the water.

Heel the boat to leeward. This cuts down further on the wetted area of the hull and keeps the sails in the correct shape. In very light winds the helm can take the weight of the boom on his shoulder while sitting to leeward. This 'opens' the leech and reduces drag.

Gusts

Change course away from the wind and try to stay with the gust as long as possible. At the same time hike out to bring the boat upright: this fans the boat forward. Then get back on or above your course and wait for the next gust.

2

Sail controls

The downhaul and outhaul should be loose. The kicking strap (vang) should be loosened completely in very light airs. The jib halyard should be no tighter than is needed to keep the jib luff just straight between the hanks. If the spinnaker is not filling, try pulling the guy and spinnaker pole towards you.

Burgee

In light winds, it's important to keep an eye on your burgee and the ripples on the water to spot changes in wind direction. Your burgee should be balanced or it will turn as the boat heels.

Reaching in strong winds

Reaching in a good breeze is the ultimate in Mirror sailing, particularly if you're flying a spinnaker. It's surprising how fast the boat can go, especially down waves. At these high speeds the helmsman and crew must act quickly, firmly and smoothly.

Adjusting the sails

Hike out hard. Pull the mainsail in as far as you can while keeping the boat level. If you are flying a spinnaker and need to turn away from the wind to keep control, do so. You can always get back on course in a lull, or take the spinnaker down before approaching the buoy.

Steering

Keep a good grip on the tiller extension. If the boat heels, turn into the wind slightly and let the sails out a little. By adjusting the mainsheet, spinnaker sheet and tiller you can keep the boat upright and go really fast. You will need to make an adjustment at least every couple of seconds.

Try to steer down waves as much as possible. As a wave picks up the boat, turn away from the wind and surf down the wave.

Trim

Both the helmsman and crew should hike nearer the stern; this lets the bow of the boat come up and skim over the water – this is *planing*. (The bow wave moves towards the stem.)

Gusts

Don't let a gust slew the boat round into the wind. If you do, the quick turn will capsize you. As the gust hits, let the sails out slightly and turn 10° to 20° away from the wind. This lets the boat 'ride with the punch'. Try to keep breathing, despite the spray!

If the boat rolls, pull the sails in and use your weight to 'dampen' the roll. Check that the centreboard is half up.

In a real squall, keep on a reach with most of the sails flapping. If you are caught with the spinnaker up, turn onto a run. Get the spinnaker down before you come back onto a reach.

Sail controls

In strong winds, all sail controls should be tight.

8 BEATING

Beating in a Mirror, particularly in a blow, is one of the most satisfying parts of sailing. You are, literally, beating the wind, which is trying to push you back.

What is beating?

A boat cannot sail straight from A to B (Figure 8.1). The sail will flap, and the boat will be blown backwards. The only way is to beat – to sail a zigzag course at an angle of about 45° to the wind.

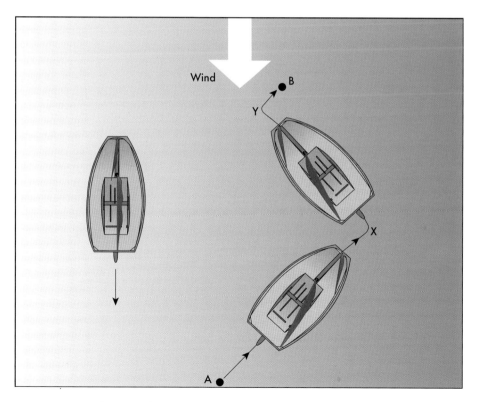

8.1 You can't sail straight from A to B – you have to beat.

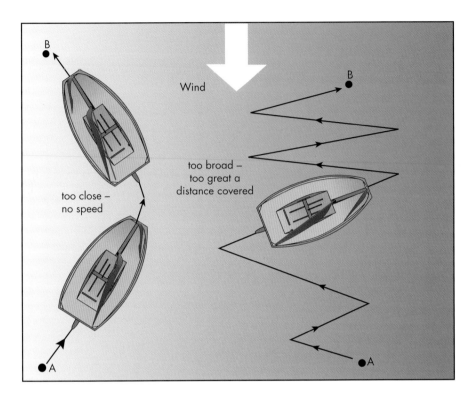

8.2 Errors of beating.

Adjusting the sails

When beating in medium or light winds there is no need to adjust the sheets. Keep them pulled in, and concentrate on using the tiller to keep the boat at the proper angle to the wind. Even though the jibsheet is cleated, the crew should keep the loose part in their hand so they can release it in a gust.

Steering

To beat, pull in the mainsheet and jibsheet firmly, hike out, and steer as close to the wind as you can. The course is a compromise: if you steer too close to the wind you slow down, even though you are pointing closer to B. If you steer too far from the wind, you go faster, but are pointing well away from B (Figure 8.2).

The simplest check on your course is to watch the front of the jib. Turn towards the wind until the jib begins to back, then turn back until it just stops flapping. You are now on course. Repeat this every few seconds – both to check your course, and because the wind constantly changes its direction. The telltales on the jib, should be streaming on both sides of the sail. If the windward one drops, turn away from the wind; if the leeward one drops turn towards the wind.

At points X and Y in Figure 8.1 the boat tacks through about 90°. Tacking is discussed on pages 51–57.

Wind

The tension of the sheets is important. In medium winds, pull in the mainsheet firmly. In light and in very strong winds, you will need to play the mainsheet in and out a little.

When the jib is sheeted to the gunwale the crew pulls the jibsheet tight except in very light winds. If inboard sheeting is used the crew pulls in the jib tight, then releases about 2cm (0.79 in.). The jib may 'backwind' the mainsail, that is, push air onto the leeward side of the mainsail: watch the front of the mainsail which will appear to flap. If this happens, ease the jibsheet or try lowering the jib tack to open the slot between jib leech and mainsail.

Trim

In flat water, sit forward with the centre of gravity of helmsman and crew (the midpoint of your combined weights) on a line one-third of the way back from the front edge of the thwart.

In rough seas, the helmsman sits as if planing – his aft leg close to the rear bulkhead – while the crew sits back level with the thwart.

The boat must always be sailed absolutely upright, except in the lightest of airs when it should be heeled to leeward.

Centreboard

The centreboard should always be pushed right down when beating.

Gusts

The water turns dark as a gust approaches. As the gust hits you, hike out hard and turn into the wind a few degrees. If the boat still heels, let the mainsail out a little. When the boat has picked up speed, pull the sail in again. When the gust has passed, move your weight inboard and adjust your course as necessary.

Windshifts

The wind constantly alters in direction. However, some changes are larger and/or last longer. These are windshifts, and it is vital you spot them and react to them when racing. Windshifts are discussed on page 109.

Sail controls

The sail should be set flatter than when reaching or running.

The kicking strap (vang) should be 'normal' or, in strong winds, tighter than 'normal'.

The downhaul should be tight enough to keep the greatest camber in the mainsail two-fifths of the way back from the mast. There should be a few horizontal creases in the front of the mainsail.

The stronger the wind, the more tension you need on the outhaul: if you're overpowered, pull the outhaul tighter. In choppy water ease the outhaul slightly to put more curve in the bottom of the sail – this provides more power to get over the waves. You will not then be able to steer so close to the wind, but the extra speed more than compensates for the extra distance sailed. Try to get a compromise setting according to wind strength and wave conditions. It's a good idea to mark the settings on the boom alongside the outhaul slide, so that you can find the right setting more easily.

Going faster

Most races start with a beat and it's essential to get to the first mark well up in the fleet. Here are some points to watch and some ideas to try:

- Keep the boat absolutely upright.

- Keep the mainsheet pulled in tight except in very light and very strong winds.

- Hike as hard as you can. Only let the mainsail out as a last resort.

- Watch the front of the jib like a hawk. Keep altering course so the jib just doesn't flap (so the telltales stream on both sides).

- Don't slam the bow into waves – lean back to lift the bow.

- Tack on windshifts.

- Keep a good lookout for other boats.

Beating in light winds

Aim for speed rather than steering very close to the wind. Keep an eye on the water and on your burgee to spot wind and windshifts.

Adjusting the sails

Pull in the mainsheet gently so the boom is as close to the centreline as possible but the leech is still open. The jibsheet should also be a little looser than normal. Most people make the mistake of pointing the boat too close to the wind in very light airs, so lay off and aim for speed. When a gust comes, let the mainsheet out a little; as the boat gathers speed, pull the mainsheet back in – but not too tight.

Steering

Hold the tiller extension gently. Watch the front of the jib and the telltales and steer as close to the wind as you can without the jib flapping. You will find you need to alter course every few seconds to keep 'on the wind'.

Trim

Sit forward in flat water until the bow is buried about 5cm(2 in.) and heel the boat to leeward. Both actions cut down the wetted area of the hull.

Sail controls

Set the kicking strap just tight enough to stop the boom lifting. It shouldn't pull it down. If you have telltales at the batten pockets, they should all stream horizontally (with sufficient wind). If the middle batten telltale doesn't stream, then there is too much tension on the leech of the main – either the mainsheet or kicking strap is too tight.

The downhaul should be fairly slack. Wrinkles up the luff in very light winds are okay.

The sail outhaul should be fairly tight to flatten the bottom of the sail in very light winds.

Beating in strong winds

In these conditions both the wind and the waves tend to stop the boat. You must not let this happen because you can only steer when the boat is moving – so speed through the waves is your main aim.

Adjusting the sails

Pull on lots of kicking strap (vang). This bends the mast, reducing the curve in the main sail. Then play the mainsheet, centering the boom as much as you can while keeping the boat upright.

In very strong winds the boat may stop if you use this technique. Ease the mainsheet a little and as soon as the bow is pushed away from the wind, ease the jib a little and 'reach' to windward. As speed is increased, point higher, pulling in the main and jibsheets.

Steering over waves

Try to steer so the boat has an easy passage over the waves. As the bow goes up a wave, push the tiller away a little. Pull the tiller as the bow reaches the crest, and turn away down the back of the wave. Repeat this for each wave – you will find you're moving the tiller all the time. Keep hiking as hard as you can.

Trim

In larger waves, the helmsman moves back, between the thwart and aft buoyancy compartment, and the crew sits level with the middle of the thwart; this lets the bow ride over the waves more easily. Try leaning towards the stern as the boat goes up a wave, and forwards as it goes down. Photo 3 shows perfect technique.

Hiking

Your body weight provides the power to get to windward. The more you hike, the faster you go. Adjust the toestraps so you're comfortable. It's easier to lever yourselves back into the boat if the toestraps are low in the cockpit; but they should be high enough so you can get your feet under them quickly.

Centreboard

In very strong winds, rake the centreboard aft in the case. (This moves he centre of effort back and balances the rudder.)

Gusts

Let the sheets out as much as is necessary to keep the boat upright and moving.

Sail controls

The kicking strap (vang), downhaul and outhaul should all be bar tight.

Beating – some common mistakes

- Mirrors, like all dinghies, sail fastest when dead upright. Both helmsman and crew seem to have forgotten to hike in photo 4.

- The main halyard is too loose in photo 5 – this is causing the horrible creases in the mainsail. Rigging like this brings tears to every sailmaker's eyes.

- The helmsman is pointing too close to the wind – or 'pinching' in photo 6.

9 TACKING

What is tacking?

The boat in the diagram is beating with the sails on the port side (a). The boat turns into the wind (b), and keeps turning until it is beating with the sails on the starboard side (c). The turn is called a tack.

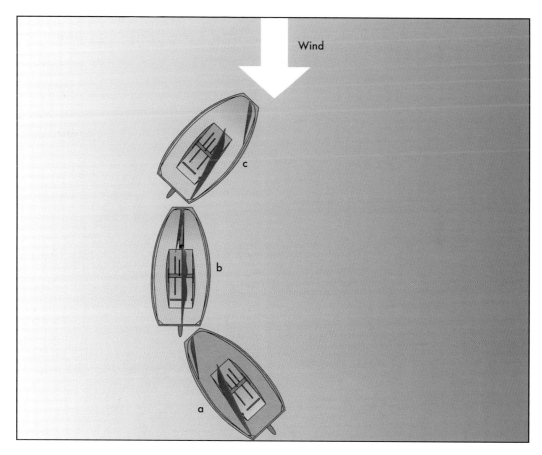

9.1 A tack.

Six steps to a good tack – helm

1. *Get some speed.* Hike extra hard to get the boat moving as fast as possible. You will need this speed to turn 'through' the wind and waves. Warn the crew that you're going to tack ('Ready about' is the traditional phrase). Let the boat heel a little to leeward (which helps you steer).

2. *Turn.* Still hiking, and with the sheets still pulled in, push the tiller away from you. Push gently at first, then a little harder. Shout 'Lee-oh' to the crew. Keep the tiller pushed over until step 5.

3. *Change hands.* Clamp the mainsheet under the thumb of the hand holding the tiller extension. You now have both sheet and extension in your 'back' hand. Grab the tiller extension with your 'front' hand. Lift your 'back' hand off the extension, holding the sheet. In this way you change hands on the sheet and tiller without letting go of either. Swivel the tiller extension round forwards.

4. *Cross the boat.* As the boom comes over, dive across the boat facing aft, ducking as you go under the boom! Keep the boat turning as you do so.

5. *Straighten up.* As you land on the new side, begin to straighten up. Don't let the boat spin round too far (onto a reach) – you're trying to get to windward. You should turn through about 90°.

6. *Go.* Pull in the sheet and hike out on the new side.

The crew's job is described on the opposite page.

Roll tacking

In lighter winds, roll tacking can help you tack faster. Plenty of practice is needed to reach perfection as the combined weight of helmsman and crew must move in harmony.

Lean the boat to leeward just before you start to tack, with the mainsheet eased out a few centimetres. As you start to turn, bring the boat upright and pull the mainsheet in. This makes the sails fan the wind, pushing the boat forwards.

9

10

11

12

13

14

As the turn continues, stay on the 'old' side. The boat will start to roll on top of you. Release the mainsheet a few centimetres. When the gunwale is almost awash the helmsman and crew move gently to the 'new' windward side. Pull in the mainsheet as the boat comes upright, fanning the boat forward a second time. Photos 9–14 show a good roll tack.

Six steps to a good tack – crew

1. *Get some speed.* Hike hard to get the boat moving. Uncleat the jibsheet, but hold it in your aft hand and keep it pulled in until step 5.

2. *Grab the new jibsheet.* Take the opposite jibsheet in your front hand.

3. *Keep hiking.* Stay on the windward side as the helmsman starts to turn.

4. *Change sides.* As the helmsman lands on the 'new' side, start to cross the boat. Face aft, take the new jibsheet with you but keep the old jibsheet pulled tight. This 'backing' of the jib helps spin the boat.

5. *Pull the jib across.* As you land on the new side pay out the old jibsheet and pull in the new one.

6. *Go.* Hike out and cleat the jibsheet to it's mark. Encourage your helmsman to drive the boat faster.

Tacking with a centre mainsheet

The crew tacks in exactly the same way as with the stern mainsheet.
  The helm tacks facing forwards:

1. Get some speed.

2. Turn by pushing the tiller away.

3. Cross the boat facing forwards and land on the new side. Do not change hands. You will now have the tiller behind your back. Steer like this for a few seconds, until the boat is on course on the new tack.

4. Now you're ready to change hands on the sheet and tiller. Bring your mainsheet hand across the front of your body and grab the tiller with it. Then transfer your 'old' tiller hand to the mainsheet. Finally, swivel the tiller extension forward across your body.

Tacking – some common mistakes

- Only back the jib for a moment. If you wait too long the boat is blown round too far, and may even capsize (photo 15). Either way, your helmsman may gently point out your error!

- Forgetting to straighten up brings the boat round too far – onto a reach in this case. The wake shows how much ground has been lost to windward. This time, the crew may take the opportunity to mention the mistake!

15

16

10 RUNNING

What is running?

Both boats in the diagram are running, that is, they're sailing with the wind directly behind.

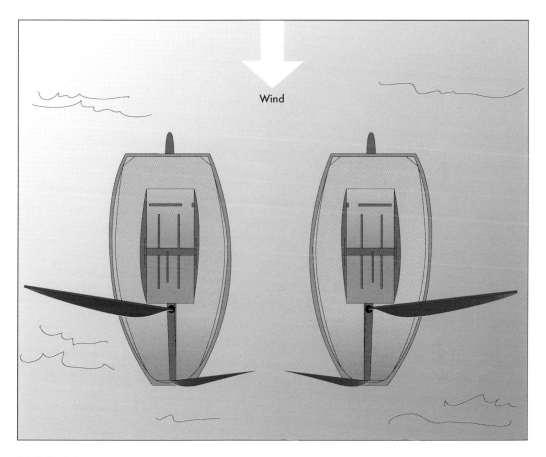

10.1 Both boats are running.

Adjusting the sails

In medium and light winds the mainsheet should be as far out as possible while the crew holds the jibsheet out on the opposite side, preferably with a jibstick. This is called goosewinging.

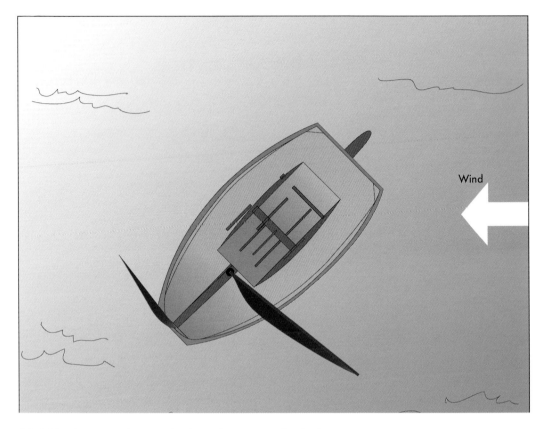

Wind

10.2 This boat is in danger of gybing. It is running by the lee.

In strong winds the helm and crew must counterbalance any rolling immediately by moving their weight or by pulling in the mainsheet a little.

Steering

Avoid violent turns – the boat is travelling fast and 'centrifugal' force may capsize you. Aim to turn smoothly and slowly.

It is vital to avoid an unexpected gybe (gybing is discussed on page 65). Watch the burgee carefully and avoid turning so that the wind is blowing from the same side as the boom. This is 'running by the lee' – the wind is able to get behind the mainsail and flip it across. If you find yourself in this position, turn quickly so the wind blows dead behind the boat (or gybe carefully).

Trim

In light to medium winds sit forward, but slide back to lift the bow over each wave. Heel the boat to windward to reduce rudder drag as well as to make the boat more responsive to tiller movement. This is called kiting.

The boat is least likely to roll if the helm and crew sit on opposite sides of the boat. Personally I prefer to sit to leeward while my crew sits to windward.

Centreboard

In light and medium winds pull the centreboard up so that only a few centimetres are in the water, to reduce drag. In very strong winds, leave the centreboard at least half down to dampen rolling. Pushing the board down also lets the crew move more freely.

Gusts

Keep going, even in strong gusts. Don't let the gust turn the boat around into the wind – keep a straight course. If the boat rolls increase the tension on the kicking strap and pull in the mainsheet. If the boat heels away from you, let the mainsheet out. If it heels towards you, pull the mainsheet in.

Sail controls

The kicking strap (vang) should be 'normal' except in light winds when it should be slacker than normal. In both cases adjust the kicker so it just stops the leech twisting.

The downhaul should be loose; aim for a lot of curve in the sail. The outhaul should be fairly tight so you can just get your fist between the sail and the boom.

Going faster

You can often gain a good number of places on a run, particularly if you are towards the back of the fleet and the wind comes up. Those in front are at your mercy because you can blanket them from the wind. Here are some points to watch and ideas to try:

- Let the mainsheet out as far as possible.

- If you aren't using a spinnaker, use a jibstick to hold the jib out on the opposite side to the mainsail.

- Make sure you have the centreboard well up to reduce drag.

- Fly the spinnaker (using a spinnaker is discussed in Part 2).

- Heel the boat to windward until the 'pull' on the tiller stops and you have neutral helm. You can now steer the boat by heel – if you heel it towards you the boat will turn away from you and vice versa.

- When a gust comes, run deeper downwind with it. Try to stay with the gust as long as possible. If you see a gust to one side of the course, sail over to it and then ride it. Wind is power!

- Try to surf on waves as much as you can. Sheet in a little as the boat accelerates down each wave.

Running in light winds

Steering

Use the tiller as little as possible. Try to balance the boat by heeling to windward so that the boat sails straight without the helmsman holding the tiller. Try to keep absolutely still.

Trim

Both helmsman and crew should be sitting in front of the thwart on opposite sides of the boat. One should hold the boom out while the other goosewings the jib. Only a few centimetres of centreboard need be in the water. If there's enough wind to fill the sails, heel the boat to windward. In very light winds, heel the boat to leeward.

Sail controls

The kicking strap should be just firm enough to prevent the boom lifting. This allows the mast to straighten and puts more curve into the sail. The downhaul should be loose, but the outhaul can be fairly tight.

Running in strong winds

Steering

Be prepared to make corrections immediately if a wave pushes the boat off course. It is essential that the rudder blade is near vertical to reduce leverage on the tiller.

Try to sail down the waves. As a wave comes up behind, turn away from the wind and surf on the wave. Be very careful not to turn so far that you gybe.

Trim

The centre of gravity of helmsman and crew should be at least 20cm behind the aft edge of the thwart. Move back still further if there is a risk of burying the bow into the wave ahead. A spinnaker stabilizes the boat, once it is up and filled; the boat need not be heeled to windward as much when flying a spinnaker.

Sail controls

All controls should be bar tight.

Centreboard

Keep the centreboard half down; this helps prevent rolling.

Running – some common mistakes

- Heel the boat slightly to windward, not to leeward (photo 2).

- In medium or light winds, sit forward. Note the turbulence caused by the stern digging into the water (photo 3).

- The jib is doing nothing. Goosewinging it will bring it out from behind the mainsail into some 'clean' air (photo 4).

- The kicking strap should be tightened to stop the boom lifting skywards and reduce twist (photo 5).

11 GYBING

What is gybing?

In the diagram, boat (a) is running with the mainsail on the starboard side. The helmsman turns through a small angle (b). The wind forces the mainsail out to the port side of the boat (c). The turn is called a gybe.

Why is gybing difficult?

Gybing is the hardest sailing manoeuvre. Unlike tacking, the wind pushes on the sail throughout the turn. The boat is moving at high speed, so is very sensitive to tiller movements. A miscalculation results in the boat rolling – with the sails 'edge on' there's not much to dampen the roll and you tend to take an involuntary dip.

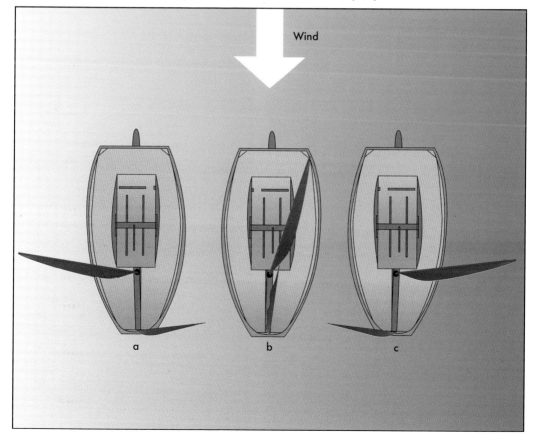

11.1 Gybing.

Decide when you want to gybe, and then do it! The best moment is when the boat is moving fast down a wave – because you're travelling away from the wind, the 'push' on the sail is lessened.

Gybing with a spinnaker is described in Part 2.

Six steps to a safe gybe – helm

1. *Get ready.* Warn the crew (shout 'Stand by to gybe') and check that he has pushed down the centreboard. Turn the boat until the wind is almost directly behind.

2. *Pull in the mainsheet.* Pull in an arm's length of mainsheet and clamp it in your tiller hand. Heel the boat to windward – if you let it heel to leeward, you can't turn.

3. *Turn.* Firmly but slowly, pull the tiller towards you. Shout 'Gybe-oh' to your crew.

4. *Cross* the boat. As the boom comes over, cross the boat facing aft. Don't forget to duck! As you move across, keep the mainsheet in your tiller hand.

5. *Steer.* As you land on the new side, pull the tiller towards you. This stops the boat turning through too large an angle. Let the mainsheet slide through your fingers so the boom can go right out.

6. *Change* hands. Grab the tiller extension with your aft hand, keeping the mainsheet in your front hand. If the boat rolls, pull in the mainsheet for a few seconds and move inboard as necessary.

As you gain confidence, try changing hands on the mainsheet and tiller extension as you are midway through the gybe.

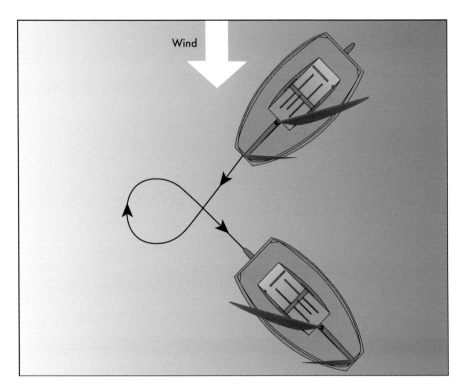

Wind

11.2 Wearing round.

Gybing in very strong winds

In very strong winds a capsize may be inevitable. If you can't pull the mainsheet in on the run, it's better to wear round. This involves turning through 360° as shown in Figure 11.2. Do this with the centreboard down. Pull in the mainsheet and spin the boat around fast.

Six steps to a good gybe – crew

1. *Lower the centreboard fully.* If you forget to do this you'll be trapped on the wrong side of the centreboard and will probably capsize.

2. *Uncleat the jibsheet.* The jib is best left flapping during the gybe, so uncleat the jibsheet and let it go.

3. *Grab the new jibsheet.* Take the opposite jibsheet in your aft hand so you're ready to adjust the sail after the gybe.

4. *Pull the kicking strap.* As the boom starts to move, use your forward hand to pull it across by the kicking strap.

5. *Cross the boat.* The wind will suddenly get behind the mainsail and flip the boom across. As it does so, duck underneath and cross the boat.

6. *Trim the jib.* Pull in the new jibsheet as much as is needed to fill the jib. Use your weight to stabilize the boat.

Gybing with a centre mainsheet

The crew gybes in the same way as above.

The helmsman gybes facing forwards:

1. Get ready, as before.

2. Pull in the mainsheet, and heel the boat to windward.

3. Turn by pulling the tiller towards you. Shout 'Gybe-oh' to your crew.

4. Cross the boat as the boom comes over, facing forwards. Keep the tiller and mainsheet in your 'old' hands.

5. Land on the new side, pulling the tiller towards you for a moment so the boat straightens up. Let the mainsheet slide out so the boom goes right out.

6. Steer with the tiller behind your back.

7. Bring the mainsheet to your tiller hand and grab it.

8. Transfer the old tiller hand to the mainsheet.

9. Finally, take the tiller extension across your body.

How not to gybe

In this gybe (photos 7 and 8), everything goes wrong:

The crew has forgotten to push down the centreboard. The helmsman turns viciously without pulling in any mainsheet.

Too late, the crew realizes he's trapped to leeward by the centreboard. The helmsman has straightened up too late – the boat has spun round almost onto a reach... with the inevitable result. The crew hasn't helped by pulling in the new jibsheet; the jib is pulling the boat over even quicker. But perhaps he's using the sheet as a lifeline!

12 CAPSIZING

Everyone capsizes. Indeed, if you don't capsize sometimes, you're probably not really trying!

Never leave the boat (to swim for the shore, for example). The hull will support you almost indefinitely – it has enough buoyancy inside to float even if the hull is punctured – and is more easily spotted than a swimmer.

The helm levers the boats uprights...   ...while the crew is scooped up to leeward.

The crew gives the helm a hand...   ...and pulls him aboard.

The boat will tip one of two ways: to leeward, or to windward (which is less pleasant).

Avoiding a capsize to leeward

- Watch for gusts.
- Keep the sheets in your hands at all times. Let them out if a gust strikes.
- Hike in strong winds.
- On a reach or run, don't let the boat turn fast into the wind.
- In very strong winds, avoid pulling the spinnaker up and down on a reach. Instead, turn onto a run while you are raising or lowering it.
- If a gust hits you on a spinnaker reach, pull the spinnaker to windward to make it flap and lose power.

Avoiding a capsize to windward

- Be ready to move your weight inboard in lulls.
- Pull in the sheets rapidly if the boat rolls to windward.
- On a reach or run, avoid turning fast away from the wind.
- When running under spinnaker, pull it to leeward as the boat rolls to windward.

Righting the boat

When the inevitable happens, try to turn around so that you are facing 'uphill'. One of you may be able to scramble over the gunwale onto the centreboard and pull the boat upright again, diving into the cockpit at the last minute. If you both fall in, then follow the procedure below:

1. The crew swims to the stern, while the helm swims around the stern of the boat to the centreboard, holding the mainsheet as a lifeline.

2. The helm holds the centreboard, stopping the boat turning upside down; the crew moves forward and pushes the centreboard right down and throws a jibsheet over the top of the hull to the helm. The crew then lies in the water on the leeward side of the boat.

3. The helm pulls himself onto the centreboard, using the jibsheet to help him.

4. As the boat comes upright, the crew is scooped on board.

5. If the helm is quick, he can also get aboard as the boat comes upright. If not, the crew can pull him in over the stern.

Tidy the gear inside the cockpit and get sailing as soon as possible. There should be very little water in the cockpit: if there is, the self-bailer will soon get rid of it.

A capsize is made worse if the rudder comes adrift. Make sure the rudder retaining clip is adjusted properly before you go afloat.

If the boat turns completely upside down, the helm should climb on top; he can then pull the boat onto its side, using the centreboard as a lever (make sure you bring the mast up to leeward of the hull). Then right the boat as described above.

Some boats have a stirrup fixed through a hole in the stern to help you climb onto the upturned hull, or to climb back into the righted boat.

In shallow water, don't let the boat turn upside down or the gaff may snap.

If the gaff gets stuck in mud, stand on the centreboard close to the hull and gently bounce up and down to free it.

13 LANDING

The way you land will depend on the direction of the wind relative to the shore. Landing badly can do a good deal of damage to the boat (and even to yourselves); always remember, for instance, to pull up your self-bailer and to undo your rudder downhaul (if you have one) in good time.

Landing with the wind along the shore

This is the easiest wind direction for landing.

1. Sail slowly towards the shore as shown in Figure 13.1. Control the boat's speed with the sheets, letting them out as you approach to slow the boat down.

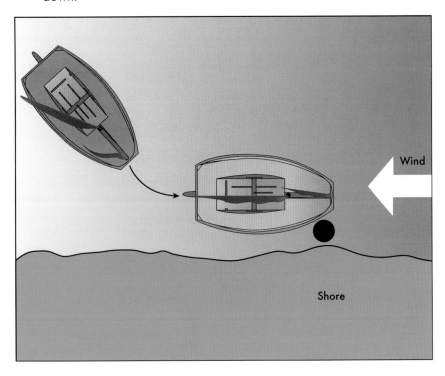

13.1 Landing with the wind along the shore.

2. At the last minute, take out the centreboard and turn into the wind.

3. One of you steps into the water on the shore side of the boat, holding it as near the bow as possible.

4. Make sure the sheets are free.

5. Pull down the sails.

Landing with an offshore wind

Beat in towards the shore. On the approach leg A, control the speed with the sheets. At the last moment, take out the centreboard, and turn the boat into the wind. The crew steps into the water as near the bow as possible; then proceed as above.

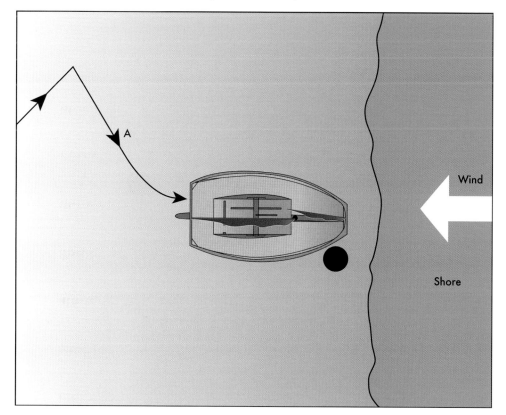

13.2 Landing with an offshore wind.

Landing with an onshore wind

This is the most difficult direction for landing because the wind is pushing you onshore fast. Unless the waves are very big, land as follows:

1. Sail parallel to the shore, about 50m(165 ft) out.

2. Turn into the wind (B) and lower the mainsail.

3. Point the boat towards the shore and let it drift in. Control the speed with the jib. If you are still going too fast, trail a leg in the water as a brake.

4. At the last minute, take out the centreboard. The crew steps into the water and holds the boat.

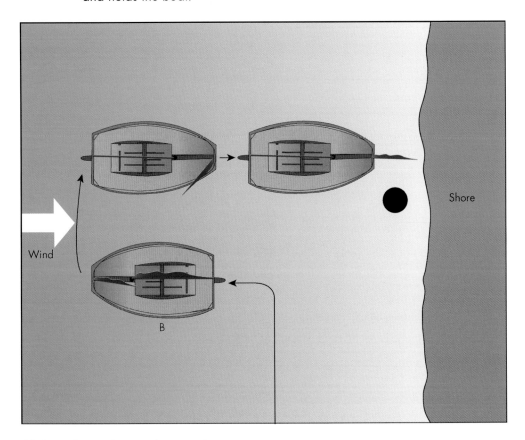

13.3 Landing with an onshore wind.

Landing in very shallow water

Come in slowly. Lift up the rudder blade and centreboard in good time and step into the water early.

Landing in big waves and an onshore wind

The method described above won't work in very large waves, because of the danger of one rolling the boat over. Use the following technique instead:

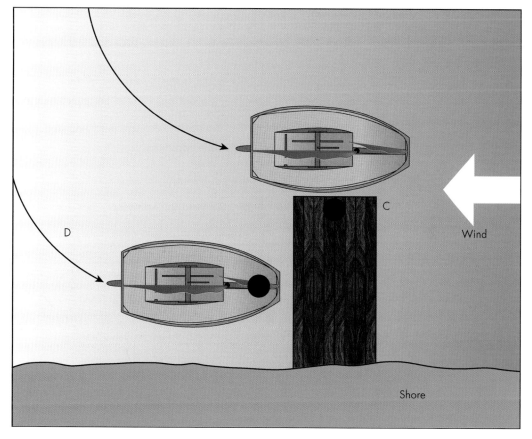

13.4 Landing at a jetty.

1. While well offshore, undo the rudder downhaul and hold it in your tiller hand. The rudder blade will come up when it hits the beach. Don't pull up the blade – you need all the control you can get. Pull the centreboard three-quarters up.

2. As you get near the beach, choose the smallest wave you can find and surf full speed on it towards the beach. Keep the bow pointing straight at the shore. Sit one on either side of the boat, well back to let the bow ride up the beach. As the boat grounds, the crew whips out the centreboard. Jump out and drag the boat up the beach. Owch!

Landing at a jetty

Sail towards the jetty slowly, controlling your speed with the sheets. Turn into the wind at the last moment (Figure 13.4).

If the 'ideal' position C is occupied, follow course D. As the boat turns into the wind, the crew goes forward and grabs the jetty. He can get onto it and tie up while the helmsman lowers the sails.

The Spinnaker

Setting up the spinnaker gear

Hoisting the spinnaker

Trimming on a reach

Trimming on a run

Gybing with a self-launching pole

Lowering the spinnaker

14 SETTING UP THE SPINNAKER GEAR

Flying downwind with the kite up is one of the great pleasures of Mirror sailing. However, you won't get very far unless the gear works properly. There are enough ways to foul up without having something jam or break.

The chute and sock

The sock shown in photo 1 has a horseshoe-shaped mouth and a full-length tube. The advantage of this is that the spinnaker is fully contained and so can't escape. Also, there are no fixings into the deck (the aft end of the sock is fixed to the shroud chainplate).

The disadvantages are the friction between kite and sock and the way the sock gets in the crew's way.

A half-length net sock is better, with a ring-and-elastic arrangement to double the spinnaker under it (photo 2). This does of course need screwing to the deck.

The chute is on the port side so that, on making the usual rounding of the windward mark to port, the spinnaker is hoisted to leeward.

The continuous halyard/downhaul

One piece of rope acts as the halyard and the downhaul. Let's follow its path in photos 3–12.

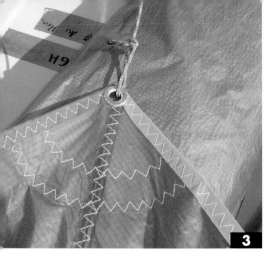

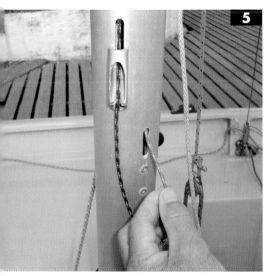

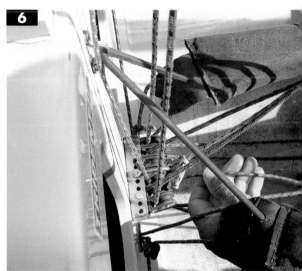

- Tie the halyard to the head of the spinnaker with a long bowline (photo 3). This keeps the head of the sail away from the mast and out of the mainsail's shadow. A mast crane is even more effective at achieving this.

- The halyard goes through a block on the mast (photo 4). (Wash this often with fresh water to prevent sticking.)

- It emerges through a slit in the mast (photo 5) . . .

- . . . and passes round a block on the forward bulkhead (the rope in Peter's hand in photo 6).

- Next it goes through a fairlead and cleat under the thwart (photo 7). The fairlead keeps the rope near the cleat.

- It now passes to a turning block at the base of the spinnaker sock, and up through the sock (photos 8, 9 and 10).

- Finally, it goes through the hole in the retrieval patch on the sail, through a bobble and is then knotted (photo 11).

Note that the downhaul rope is rigged in front of the spinnaker (photo 12). When you pull down the sail, this helps prevent it falling over the bow.

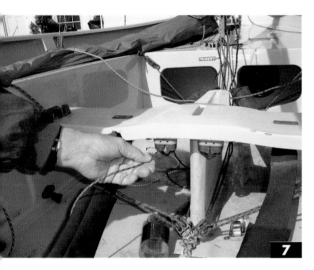

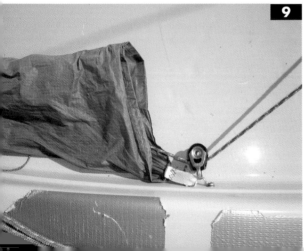

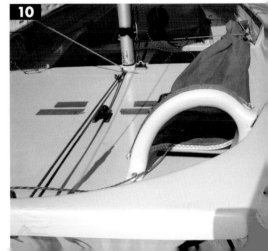

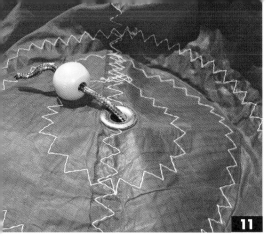 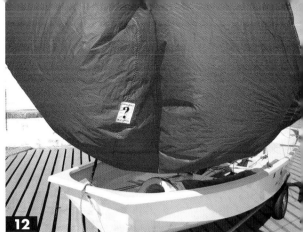

Note also that there has to be enough slack in the rope for you to be able to pull up the sail without the tension pulling it down at the same time.

The continuous sheet/guy

On the Mirror the spinnaker sheets, which control the lower corners of the sail, are continuous.

To avoid misunderstanding, when the sail is flying the sheet controlling the pole end of the spinnaker is called the guy. The sheet controlling the free-flying corner of the spinnaker is called the sheet. Don't get confused: when you gybe and transfer the pole to the new corner, the old sheet becomes the new guy and vice-versa!

Attach the sheet to one end of the spinnaker as shown in photos 13, 14 and 15.

1. Pass the end through the cringle (hole) in the sail and tie a thumb knot.

2. Then tie another thumb knot around the rope.

3. Pull tight. This arrangement means the sail can lie right against the jaws of the pole.

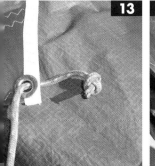  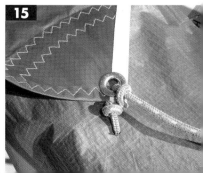

4. Pass the sheet through the ring of the fixed barber-hauler (photo 16). This prevents the sheet going over the end of the boom when the sail flaps.

5. Note the guy cleat (photo 17). When the guy is on this side of the boat the rope goes through this cleat to hold the pole down and keep the guy out of the crew's way. Of course, there's an identical cleat on the opposite side of the boat.

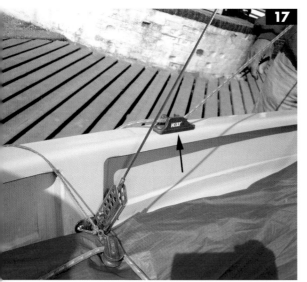

6. The rope passes round a turning block well aft (photo 18). Ideally this would be at the back of the boat, but because of the problem of the sheet getting caught over the boom, the block is usually stationed above the aft bulkhead.

7. Next is a turning block at the base of the shroud (photo 19).

8. The sheet runs across the boat, and the arrangement on the other side is symmetrical.

When you have rigged the sheet, it's important to check that it is **running outside everything**. If there isn't too much wind, hoist the kite on land (photo 20) to make sure there are no tangles.

The length of the sheet is critical. On a well set-up boat, as the spinnaker pole is launched it pulls out about 30cm of sheet from the sock.

20

The spinnaker pole

I'm going to describe the self-launching pole here. The one I prefer, the end-for-end pole, is described in Chapter 26, 'Setting up the boat for racing'.

Note the instructions for fitting this pole are on the Mirror website <http://www.ukmirrorsailing.com>.

The pole is retrieved by a **shock-cord retainer**. Use 5mm stretchy shock cord. (There are two types: one extends to twice the length, the other to three times. Use the latter.) The shock cord is attached to the aft end of the pole. It passes through a fairlead, round a block and into the boom (photo 21). It goes round an internal pulley near the gooseneck and back aft, exiting through the boom end (photo 22). A knot prevents it pulling back.

The pole is launched by the **launching rope**. This runs from the pole end, through a block fixed to the spinnaker pole ring on the front of the mast (photo 23), and down to a turning block and swivelling cleat (photo 24). Make the tail long enough for the helmsman to grab it if he needs to.

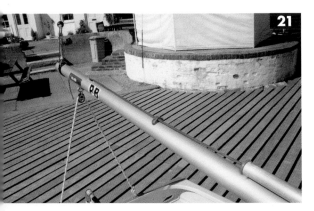

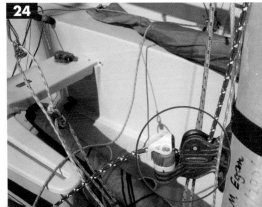

Adjust the width of the jaws at the end of the pole so the guy **just** goes in and out (photo 25).

The pole is fitted with an uphaul and a downhaul (photo 26). The **uphaul** is unsprung. It goes from the pole, over a pulley halfway up the mast (photo 27), and down to a cleat on the mast (photo 28).

The **downhaul** is rope from the pole, then elastic (photo 29). Set it up so that when the pole is raked up to its maximum, the elastic's block hits the turning block.

25

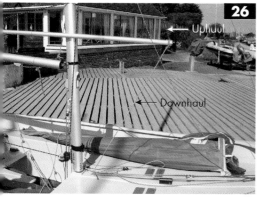

26

Uphaul

Downhaul

27

28

29

15 HOISTING THE SPINNAKER

Let off the kicking strap (vang) before you launch the kite.

Note that the ideal is for the pole to go out and the halyard to go up at the same time.

Here is how the helm and crew should synchronise:

Helm	Crew
Make the decision to hoist and say 'Hoist'. Bear away onto a broad reach. Stand up and steer with your knees. Cleat the mainsheet or stand on it.	Put the guy into the pole end. Put the guy into the windward cleat. (There should be a mark on the rope.) This prevents the sail blowing away to leeward after the hoist. Say 'Ready'.
Pull the halyard.	Pull out the pole.
Check the kite is fully up – using a mark on the rope or by looking up. On a windy day, give the crew a hand to pull in the guy.	Adjust the guy in the cleat. Grab the sheet and trim the sail. Adjust the pole height so the clews are level.

In an emergency, the helm can grab the middle of the spinnaker sheet and pull aft. This brings the whole kite in, behind the jib and mainsail, and takes the pressure out of it.

Problems with hoisting

- **The guy falls out of the pole end.** Finish the hoist but let the pole back in. Put the guy into the end, then pull out the pole again.

- **The halyard doesn't cleat.** Put a vertical mark on the thwart so you can line up the halyard and know it is being pulled through the cleat.

- **The guy falls out of the cleat on the deck.** The helm pulls on the guy while the crew cleats it.

- **There is too much pressure in the sail for you to cope.** Sail deeper, that is, bear away.

16 TRIMMING ON A REACH

While the spinnaker is up it's the crew's only responsibility. Trimming it is the most important job on the boat – a flapping kite is a killer to boatspeed.

If the kite is going to collapse, the helm should bear away to help the crew set it. (On a racing yacht the trimmers are constantly calling for the helm to do this, because it takes quite a while for them to winch in the spinnaker.)

On a close reach set the pole just off the forestay (photo 1). As the wind frees set the pole as far back as possible. It will be at right angles to the wind and the pole and mainsail boom will be roughly in line.

You also need to adjust the pole height. To point high, lower the outer end of the pole to tighten the spinnaker luff. As the wind comes aft, raise the pole. Because of the geometry, as you raise or lower the pole you need to loosen or tighten the guy.

Once the pole is set correctly, loosen the sheet until the luff of the kite begins to curl, then sheet in until the curl stops. Repeat continually.

To go fast:

1. The helm should steer to the waves.

2. Put the daggerboard down if you want height. Otherwise have it half up to reduce resistance.

3. In light winds sit forward. As you plane, sit back. The crew may have to share the helm's toestraps! On a broad reach the helm may need to sit to leeward.

17 TRIMMING ON A RUN

The crew plays the guy and sheet together – as the guy tightens the sheet slackens, and vice versa. The most efficient way to play the guy is to cleat it loosely, then pull back on the rope between the sail and the cleat.

It is worth running dead downwind in a Mirror. The pole will come back square to the boat.

As the pole comes back, the outboard end wants to go up. The main objective is to keep the clews level.

The spinnaker is the priority, but play the jib when you can.

18 GYBING WITH A SELF-LAUNCHING POLE

Gybing is mostly crew work. (But the helm needs to steer to keep the boat upright!) Here is what the crew does:

1. Put the daggerboard down (or you won't be able to cross the boat).

2. Pull the jib across to the new side and set the sheet loosely.

3. Get the boat level. You can't gybe if you are heeling.

4. Retrieve the pole and take the guy out of the pole end.

5. Put one hand on the kicking strap (vang) and the other on the guy.

6. Pull both together. The kite will float out to windward and the main boom will come across.

7. Duck under the boom.

8. Reach for the new guy.

9. Put it into the end of the pole.

10. Re-launch the pole. (Either the helm or the crew can do this.)

11. Set the pole and trim the sheet.

12. Blast off!

The helm controls the spinnaker sheet throughout the gybe, to keep things under control.

Problems with gybing

- **Capsizing!** The helm must steer to keep the boat level. Plan ahead so you don't have a boat to leeward, preventing your bearing away when you most need to. If necessary, pull the spinnaker in tight on the sheet and guy, or let the sheet go. Do everything you can to stay upright – better a bad gybe than a swim. Practise steering with your knees without the kite up. Practise strong wind gybes without a pole to give you the feel for it.

- **After the gybe, the kite blows into the jib and, being wet, sticks to it.** Pull the kite to windward before the gybe.

- **The crew gets stuck on the (new) leeward side.** Put the daggerboard down before you gybe, to make room.

19 LOWERING THE SPINNAKER

The objective is for the pole to come in as the sail is lowered.

Note that the crew needs to ease the sheets towards the end of the drop so the helm can pull the kite home into the chute.

Here is how the helm and crew should synchronise:

Helm	Crew
Bear away. Stand up. Hold the tiller between your knees. Control the mainsheet by cleating it or standing on it.	
Release the halyard. Lower it as you pull the downhaul.	Retrieve the pole onto the boom. You may need to flick the pole end if it's stuck on the mast. The guy usually comes out of the pole end. If not, give it a tug.
Keep pulling the spinnaker into the chute	Let the sheets go so the kite can be pulled in. If you have time, tidy up!

Problems on the drop

1. **The kite falls over the bow.** Pull it back up again and then drop it. The retrieval line should be in front of the spinnaker.

2. **If the jib is on the port side when you drop the kite, the jib can block off the chute.** Pull in the jib before the drop.

The elements of racing

The rules

The line start

The beat

The reach

The run

20 THE RULES

A full discussion of the rules is outside the scope of this book. For the cautious beginner, a few key rules will keep you out of trouble in most cases.

Boats meeting on opposite tacks

A boat is either on a port tack or a starboard tack. It is on a port tack if the wind is blowing over its port side. In Figure 20.1, boats A, B and C are on port tack; boats D, E and F are on starboard tack.

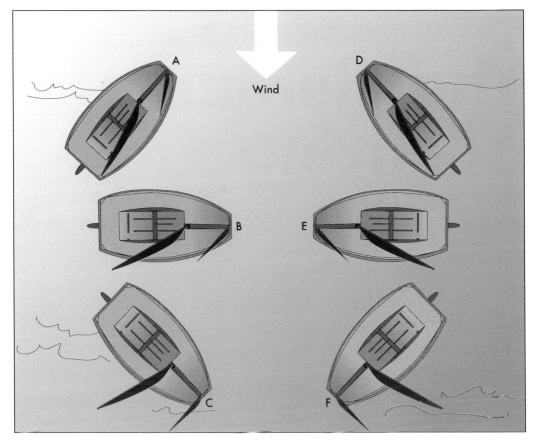

20.1 A, B and C must give way to D, E and F.

A port tack boat must keep clear of a starboard tack boat:
D, E and F have right of way over A, B and C, who must keep clear.

Boats meeting on the same tack

If the boats are overlapped (that is, if the bow of the following boat is ahead of a line at right angles to the stern of the leading boat), the following rule applies:

A windward boat shall keep clear of a leeward boat:
In Figure 20.2, G must keep clear of H, I must keep clear of J and L must keep clear of K.

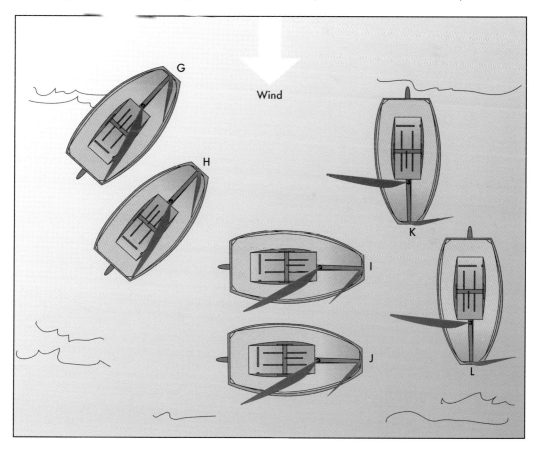

20.2 Windward keeps clear of leeward.

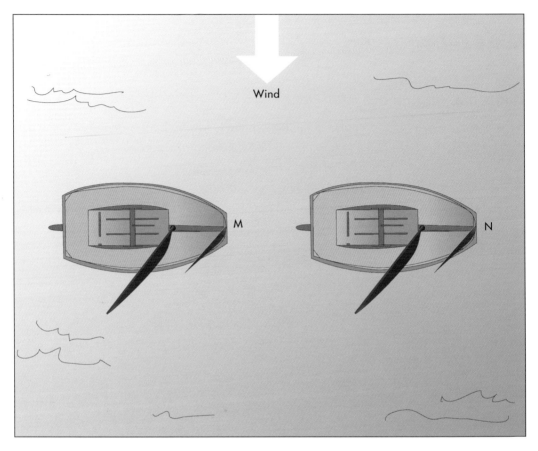

Wind

20.3 Overtaking boat keeps clear.

If the boats are not overlapped (see Figure 20.3):

A boat clear astern shall keep clear of a boat clear ahead:
M is overtaking and is not allowed to sail into the back of N.

Boats meeting at marks

The following rules apply:
An outside boat shall give each boat overlapping it on the inside room to round or pass the mark:

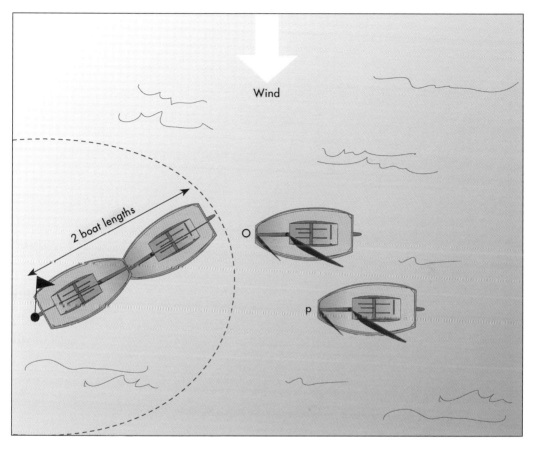

20.4 The outside boat keeps clear.

O must give P room to go round the mark on the inside. P must get his overlap on O before O's bow reaches an imaginary circle of radius two boat's lengths from the mark (see Figure 20.4).

Note that this rule does not apply at starts (see below).

Penalties

If you hit a mark, you must sail clear as soon as possible and make a 360° turn (tack, then gybe).

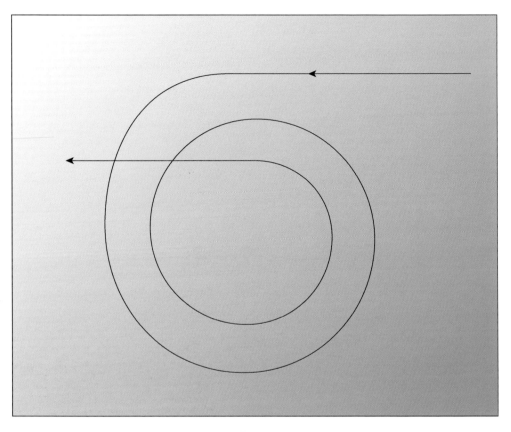

20.5 A 720° penalty turn (a Two Turns Penalty).

If you hit another boat and reckon you're in the right, protest by shouting 'Protest'. Argue your case in the protest room afterwards.

If you hit another boat and you're in the wrong, you must either retire or, if the rules allow (they usually do), make a 720° turn. In effect, you have to tack, gybe, tack again and gybe again – then sail on (see Figure 20.5).

21 THE LINE START

The start is the most important part of the race. If you get a bad start, you have to overtake everyone to win – while you're battling past the opposition, the leaders are sailing further ahead. If you get a good start, you're sailing in clear air.

How is a race started?

Most races are started on a beat. The race committee sets an (imaginary) start line, usually between the mast of the committee boat (A) and a buoy (B) (see Figure 21.1).

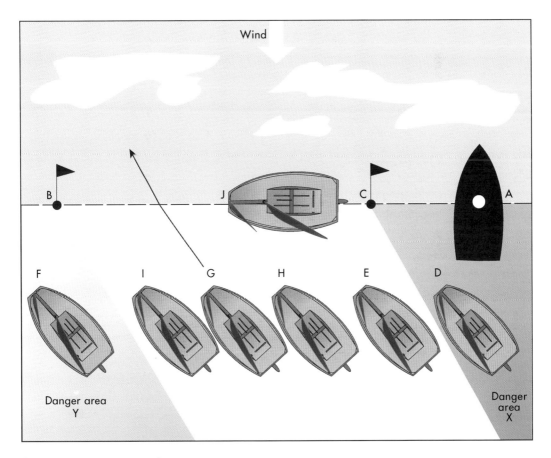

21.1 ...How to get a good start.

They often lay another buoy (C), which does not have to be on the line. Boats are not allowed to sail between C and A.

Five minutes before the start: the class flag is raised on the committee boat and a gun is fired (or a sound made).

Four minutes before the start: the Blue Peter is raised and a gun is fired.

One minute before the start: the Blue Peter is lowered and a gun is fired.

Boats must be behind the start line when the starting gun goes. Your aim is to be just behind the line, sailing at full speed, when the gun fires.

How can I get a good start?

Set your watch at the five-minute gun, and check it at the four-minute gun.

During the last few minutes, avoid the 'danger' areas X and Y (Figure 21.1). From X you cannot get on to the start line because the boats to leeward have right of way. Boat D, for example, will be forced the wrong side of buoy C. In Y you are bound to pass the wrong side of buoy B. Boat F has this problem.

Don't go too far from the line – 30 metres is plenty. A wall of boats builds up on the line in the last two minutes, and you must be in that wall. If you're behind it, not only can you not get in, but your wind is cut off by the wall.

Aim to be two boat lengths behind the line with 20 seconds to go. Control your speed by backing or flapping the jib. Keep the boat creeping forward as slowly as you can – most of the sails will be flapping. With five seconds to go, you should be one length behind the line. Free the jib, pull in the jib and mainsheets, hike out and start beating. You should cross the line just after the gun with full speed. Boat G has followed this advice.

It's important to watch out for other boats as you line up to start. G has right of way over H, but must keep clear of I. As you line up, keep turning into the wind a little. This keeps you away from the boat to leeward – it also opens up a nice 'hole' to leeward that you can sail down into at the start (for extra speed).

Don't reach down the line with 15 seconds to go like boat J. You will have no rights over G, H and I who will sail into you. If you're too early, let the sails out in good time and slow down.

Which end of the line should I start?

In diagram 21.1 the wind is at right angles to the start line. In this case it doesn't matter where you start – the middle is as good as anywhere.

Usually, however, the wind is not at right angles to the line. You can find out what it's doing by sailing down the line on a reach with the jib flapping. Adjust the mainsail so the front just flaps (see Figures 21.2 and 21.3).

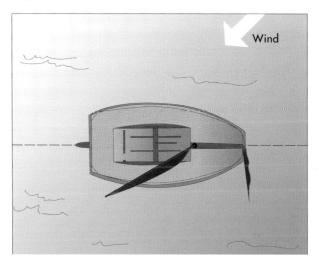

21.2 Sail towards one end of the line and tack...

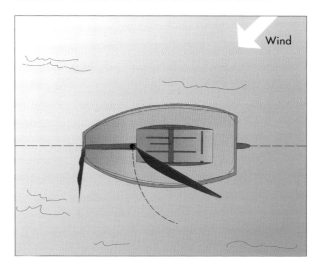

21.3 ...the starboard end of the line is favoured.

Keeping the mainsheet in the same position, tack and reach back down the line. In Figure 21.3, the mainsail will now be too far in – you will have to let the mainsheet out to make it flap. This indicates the wind is blowing from the starboard end of the line – and you should start at the starboard end.

How do I make a starboard end start?

Sail slowly, and as close to the wind as possible, so you will reach the windward end of the line with the gun (see Figure 21.4). Boats to windward have no rights and are forced out. Boats to leeward can't touch you – you are already sailing as close to the wind as possible.

How do I make a port end start?

Keep near the port end of the line (see Figure 21.5).

Aim to cross as near the buoy as possible. Tack on to port tack as soon as you can clear the fleet.

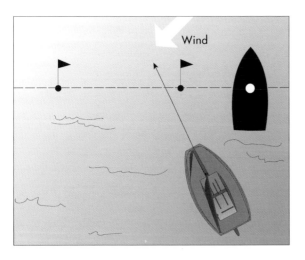

21.4 How to make a starboard end start.

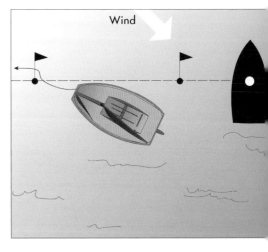

21.5 How to make a pin end start.

22 THE BEAT

After the tension of the start, it's important to settle down and concentrate on sailing hard.

What about other boats?

A boat when beating casts a 'wind shadow' – shown in Figure 22.1. It also creates an area of disturbed air to windward due to the wind being deflected by the sails; the air behind the boat is also disturbed.

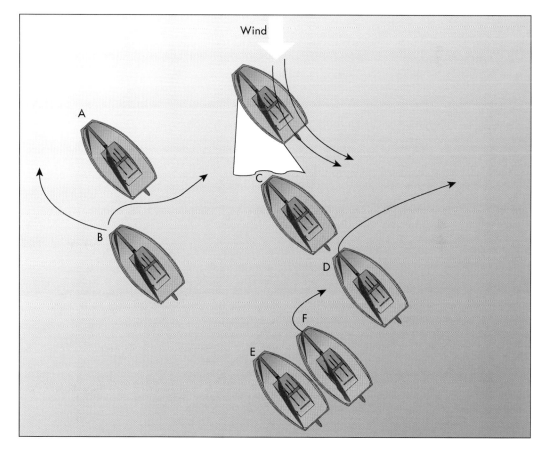

22.1 Keep your wind clear.

You should therefore avoid sailing just to windward of another boat, behind it or in its wind shadow. In the diagram, boat B should either tack or bear away to clear its wind. Boats D and F should both tack.

Which way should I go?

You may have to modify your course to take account of tides and windshifts, but your first aim should be to make reasonably long tacks to start with, shortening them as you approach the windward mark.

Don't sail into the area indicated by the shaded part of Figure 22.2 – if you do, you will have to reach in to the buoy and will lose valuable time and distance. Stay inside the lay lines – these are the paths you would sail when beating to hit the windward mark.

For safety's sake, arrange your tacks so that you come in to the mark on starboard tack. This gives you right of way over those approaching on port tack.

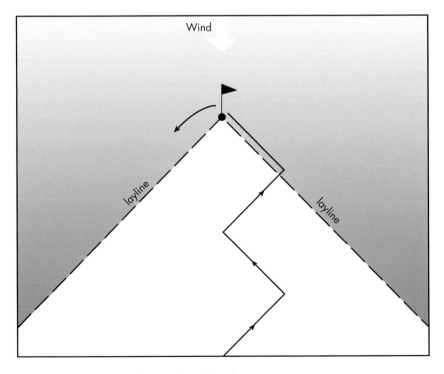

Wind

layline

layline

22.2 An ideal route to the windward mark.

Windshifts

Once you are confident at beating and can tack efficiently, you are ready to start using windshifts.

The wind constantly alters in direction about its mean. Some of the shifts are more pronounced and last longer than others – it is these that you have to spot and use.

In shifty winds, stay close to the middle of the beat. Tack each time the wind heads you (forces you to alter course away from the mark). In Figure 22.3, the boat takes no account of windshifts. Note how little progress it makes compared with the boat in Figure 22.4, which tacks each time the wind heads it.

The main problem is to differentiate between a real shift and a short-lived change in the wind. For that reason, sail on into each shift for five or ten seconds to make sure it's going to last.

If a header lasts that long, tack.

If you find yourself tacking too often, or are confused, sail on one tack for a while until you're sure what the wind is doing. Remember that you lose at least a boat's length each time you tack, so there has to be a good reason to do so.

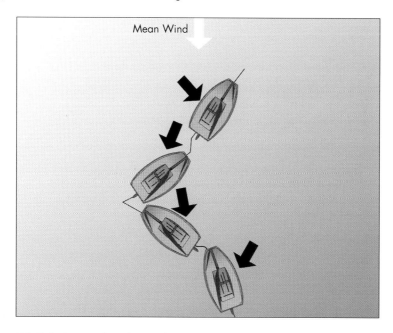

22.3 Sailing on headers is slow.

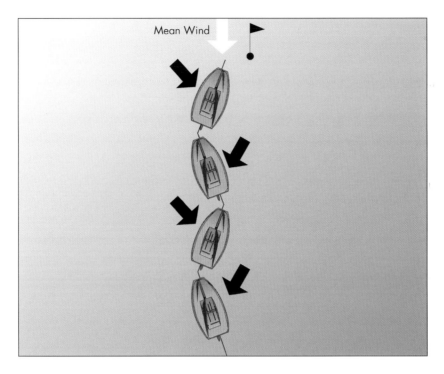

22.4 Sailing on lifts in fast.

How can I get up the beat faster?

Follow the tips for fast beating on page 45, 'Going faster'.

- Keep your wind clear.

- Watch for windshifts and use them.

- Keep near the middle of the course.

- Practise tacking.

- Get fit – you can then hike harder.

23 THE REACH

As you bear away round the windward mark, turn slowly, moving your weight back and letting out the sheets. Pull the centreboard half up as you turn.

What course should I steer?

The quickest way down the reach is a straight line from one mark to the next. However, if your rivals let you sail this course, you're lucky! The problem is that overtaking boats (for example A in Figure 23.1) push up to windward. The boats to leeward (for example B)

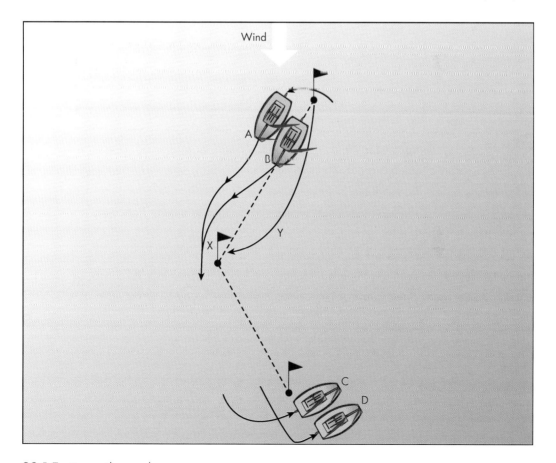

23.1 Tactics on the reach.

get nervous about their wind being stolen and steer high also. The result is that everyone sails an enormous arc (X), losing ground on the leaders.

You have to decide whether or not to go on the 'great circle'; the alternative is to sail a leeward path (Y). You have to go down far enough to avoid the blanketing effect of the boats to windward – but usually you will sail a shorter distance than they do. You will also get the inside turn at the gybe mark. You can go for the leeward route on the second reach too, but this time you will be on the outside at the turn.

How can I get down the reach faster?

- Follow the tips for fast reaching on page 37, 'Going faster'.

- Keep your wind clear.

- Sail the shortest route.

- Go for the inside turn at marks.

- Use the spinnaker if the wind is on the beam or further aft. Don't use the spinnaker on a reach if you're likely to capsize!

Starting the next beat

As you approach the leeward mark, tighten the downhaul and outhaul and push down the centreboard. Steer round the mark so that you leave it very close (like boat C). Don't come in to the mark close (like boat D) or you'll start the beat well to leeward of your rivals.

24 THE RUN

In strong winds, take your time as you bear away to a run. Pull the centreboard half up, sit back and adjust the sheets as you turn. If the boat starts to roll, steer a straight course and pull in the mainsheet a little. Continue to bear away when the boat is under control.

What course should I steer?

The quickest route is a straight line to the leeward mark (see Figure 24.1).

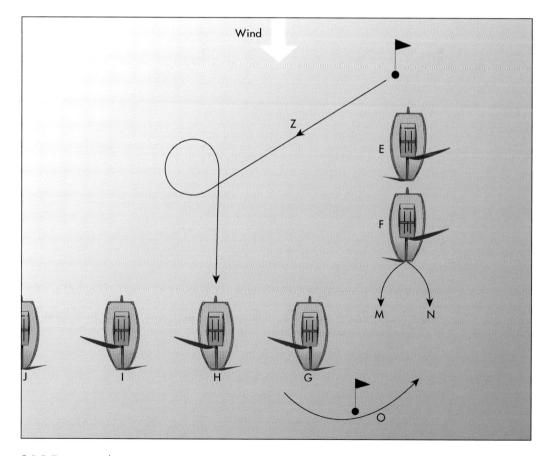

24.1 Tactics on the run.

In very strong winds, you may not be able to control the boat a straight downwind run. An alternative is to follow course Z, wearing round (see page 68) rather than gybing at the midpoint.

The presence of other boats may also prevent your steering a straight course. Boat F is blanketed by boat E – it can escape by steering to one side (course M or N). Other things being equal, N would be better since it gives the inside turn at the next mark.

Boat E is correct to blanket F in this way. E can attack from a range of up to four boat's lengths; it can sail right up behind F, turning to one side at the last moment to overtake. E must, of course, keep clear of F during this manoeuvre.

Watch out for boats still beating, especially when running on port tack. Alter course in good time to avoid them – a last minute turn could capsize you.

What about crowding at the leeward mark?

It often happens that several boats arrive at the leeward mark together. The inside berth is the place to aim for – H, I and J have to give G room to turn inside them. If you're in J's position, it's better to slow down and wait to turn close to the buoy rather than sail round the outside of the pack. Try to anticipate this situation, and slow down and move across to the inside in good time. Try to get G's position.

As you get near the leeward mark, tighten the downhaul and push the centreboard down. Turn slowly and aim to leave the mark close (course O). You will need to pull in a good length of mainsheet as you round this mark – pull it in with your front hand, then clamp it under the thumb of your tiller hand while you grab the mainsheet to pull in the next length.

How do I get down the run faster?

Follow the 'Going faster' tips on page 62.

- Keep your wind clear.

- Go for the inside turn at the leeward mark.

- Use the spinnaker.

Masterclasses

Mental and physical fitness

Setting up the boat for racing

Boatspeed

Advanced boat handling

Advanced crewing

Race preparation

Travelling to an event

Strategy

Parents, coaches, be your own coach

25 MENTAL AND PHYSICAL FITNESS

Sailing is an endurance sport. You are often on the water from 10am to 5pm or later, and hiked out for much of that time. In between there are bursts of aerobic activity such as starting, tacking and gybing. No wonder you need a lie-down after racing!

The fitter you are the better you can concentrate. If you are preoccupied with the pain in your legs, you're not really focused on climbing the wave in front.

Your own experience will tell you what hurts after a race – maybe your legs or stomach muscles – and that is what you want to work on in the gym.

At the gym

Talk to your trainer. He will give you a heart rate monitor and get you to work on exercises that put you into your optimum heart rate range. (This is different for everyone.) Basically, he will advise on the three areas of exercise: burning fat, endurance conditioning, specific strength areas.

If you are a junior (10–16) keep a record of your height and stop training if you're having a growth spurt. Your bones grow and the tendons haven't caught up yet so there is a possibility of damaging them. Don't do weight training and tell your coach.

Don't train if you're injured. If you have pain, training won't do you any good. Talk to a sports physio or phone the RYA sports physio if you are in a squad. Some gentle swimming may be the best interim solution.

If you can't get to a gym

Here is a circuit that will help your mobility and flexibility. Do it twice a week and repeat each exercise six to 12 times.

1. **Compass jumps.** Stay on your toes with your feet together and jump forwards, back, sideways to the right and sideways to the left (photos 1–4).

2. **Inner leg raise.** Lie on your side. Support your upper body on your arm. Extend the leg closest to the floor and lift it towards the roof. Hold for 2 seconds. Lower it slowly (photos 5–6).

3. **Press ups.** (Photos 7–8). If you can't do them on your hands and toes, kneel down and do them on your knees and hands. But if you need a greater challenge, have your feet on a bench.

In photos 9 and 10 I have put my forefingers and thumbs together to make a diamond. Doing press ups like this exercises different muscles.

4. **Squats.** Stand upright with your feet slightly apart. Have your arms out in front of you. 'Sit down' towards a chair, but in fact hover above the seat. Keep your feet flat. Hold for 5 seconds.

5. **Pull-ups on a table.** Lie under a table. Hold the edge. Keeping your body stiff, pull up as far as you can. You will be resting on your heels.

6. **Ski training.** 'Sit' with your back against the wall, and your legs bent. Hold for 15 seconds.

7. **Shuttle runs.** Make two marks 20 metres apart. Sprint between them one way, then jog back the other way.

8. **Squat thrusts.** Get into the press-up position, with your feet together. Hop your feet forward, so your knees are near your chest. Then hop your feet back to the start position.

9. **Leg raises.** Lie on your side. Extend both legs and keep them straight. Lift the top leg towards the roof and hold for two seconds. Then bring it down slowly.

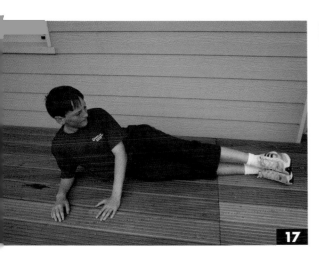

10. **Stomach curl.** Lie on your back, hands behind your head. Sit up three-quarters of the way. Slowly lie back again.

As well as this circuit you will want to do some jogging, cycling and swimming. Jog on grass to avoid hard surfaces, which can damage your knees and ankles. Wear good trainers.

Either cycle fast for 20 minutes (8 km 5 miles) or more slowly for 40 minutes (13 km 8 miles). This is good for endurance and is less likely to damage you than jogging.

Swimming is excellent exercise. Alternate one fast length with one slow length.

And while you are playing computer games, why not sit on a Swiss Ball? It is excellent exercise for your core muscles.

Drugs and drug testing

At European and World Championships you need to be aware of drug testing. It is usually inhalers that give a problem, for example, asthma inhalers. Check your formula on www.100percentme.co.uk and see if the contents of your medicine come up red or green. If red, you need to declare the inhaler before the event. If in doubt, check with the RYA doctor.

Fluid for race day

Take out at least two bottles of fluid. The idea is to drink little but frequently. Provided you do this and have salts added to the water, you shouldn't have to go to the loo too often. (Pure water tends to go straight through you, a salty mix is converted to sweat.)

I recommend a sports drink such as Lucozade Sports Drink but with extra water in it. Alternatively put one tablespoon of SIS powder in a bottle of water. Checkout science in sport.com

If you're stuck, make up a drink with pure orange juice diluted to 50% with water plus a pinch of salt. (Avoid orange juice flavourings.)

At hot venues take even more fluid, preferably in the coach boat.

Food for race day

You can snack during or between races, and will also need a packed lunch.

For snacking take energy bars such as Fruit Naturally which has nuts and cereals. Bananas are a good mix of sugar and carbohydrate. The riper the better (though you do slide further on a squashy banana!). Take some reward sweets such as Jaffa Cakes. Jelly babies are excellent because they are mainly glucose, not sugar.

For your packed lunch go for sandwiches containing food that is easy to digest such as tuna, cheese or egg. (Something like bacon takes ages to digest, taking blood to your stomach just when you want it in your muscles.) Alternatively, take pasta in a plastic container. Allow yourself a small amount of meat to make it taste better, if you must.

Think carefully about how you are going to keep the fluid and food clean – seawater is often dirty and at a recent Olympics virtually every member of the British team was sick. Use watertight containers.

Warming up

Warm up ashore to make sure you don't injure yourself afloat.

Three or four minutes of exercise and stretching will do. Repeat afloat if there is a long delay.

Try some of the following:

- A little jog.

- Stretch your arms out and swing them round and round.

- Roll your head forwards, sideways and back.

- Look left, then right.

- 'Windmill' your arms.

- Twist your torso.

- Touch your toes.

- Stretch your hamstrings. Put your leg out forwards, then partially sit down, bending forwards a little.

Warming down

Warming down is important in order to 'flush' your muscles and prevent build up of lactic acid. When you come ashore, jog to get your trolley, then concentrate on some general stretching, working on your legs and stomach.

Eating immediately you get ashore

You will need to re-carb within 30 minutes of landing. You have been running on your reserve tank and want to fill the main tank with fuel. Pasta is excellent and you can go heavier on meat now, because you aren't performing until the next day.

Mental fitness

You don't have to be mental to sail a Mirror, but it helps!

We are aiming for mental toughness, which is the ability to regain your concentration after a setback, leaving negative thoughts behind.

Things go wrong all the time in racing. After an incident there is no point in dwelling on how unfair it was, how badly the other boat behaved, or what your coach is going to say afterwards. Forget it, concentrate on the 'here and now' not the past, and get on with the race.

I try to teach people to **control the controllables, and forget the uncontrollables.**

Here are six key controllables:

1. A good knowledge of the racing rules. Read the first 25 pages of the rule book, and *The Rules in Practice* by Bryan Willis. Everything else you can look up afterwards, perhaps before a protest.

2. The sailing instructions (SIs). In a recent Mirror Southern Area Championships, 75% of the fleet sailed the wrong course. Know the SIs backwards and take them with you.

3. The wind and tide and how they affect your strategy. Work this out before you go afloat, and that's one less thing to worry about.

4. Boat preparation. You don't want to be thinking about a dodgy fitting just before a heavy weather gybe. Check everything before the event.

5. Boat handling. Sorry, you'll just have to practise this.

6. Physical fitness. Sorry again, you can't throw money at this. Get down to the gym!

And some uncontrollables are: the weather; what the other boats are doing; other boats' sails, fittings, and crew weight.

This leads to what I call the Three Cons:

- Control

- Concentration

- Confidence

These are linked, as in the diagram below. When you control the controllable, your concentration rises and so does your confidence, which helps you control the controllable.

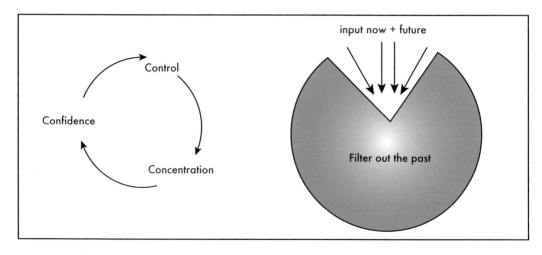

25.1

After a setback

Work out a routine in training so that when things go wrong you can drop into the routine and be mentally tough. Work out a trigger word that will reset yourself into the now – mine is 'bubblegum' but it can be any word that works for you.

After an incident it's okay to vent your anger but limit this to 30 seconds. Then you or your crew invoke the trigger word and get back to the 'here and now' and what I call the 'pizza zone of the future'(see diagram on previous page). What I mean by this is that you can receive data on what is going to be happening now and in the near future, such as waves, wind shifts and potential collisions, but filter out anything from the past or anything irrelevant like admiring yachts in the spectator fleet.

26 SETTING UP THE BOAT FOR RACING

In this section we're looking for free speed. I'm not talking about money here, rather the sort of improvement you get by doing something once – as opposed to a repetitive task like hiking which you have to do all the time.

Marking things on the boat

A brilliant sailor like Paul Elvstrom, who won five gold medals in a row, would never mark anything because he preferred to 'feel' the boat. But for us mortals, marking settings and putting on reference marks helps trimming, gives a guide to speed, enables fast settings to be repeated and may prevent arguments!

Because you'll always want to change the marks once they are there, take out black, red and blue pens. For dark sheets use whipping twine wrapped round three times and sewn through the rope.

Most control lines have a range of settings but halyards are a special case. They only have one position – up! Mark the jib halyard to show it's up and that it hasn't slipped. Use a wire main halyard with a hook rack. Set it so the head of the sail is at the black band. Check before the start of each race that it's in position. The spinnaker halyard mark is 5cm long because it doesn't matter if it's right up or down a little, and it may sometimes be an advantage to have a gap between the head and the mast. This mark is really useful – you can put your head down and pull like crazy until the mark lines up, then go straight into trimming the sail.

All other sheets and control lines have a range of settings, depending on the wind. You should be adjusting them **all the time**. Note that changing one affects all the others – though it doesn't mean you have to adjust them too. For example, raising the jib tack alters the sheeting angle and also tightens the jibsheet (which may or may not be what you want). Just be aware of what is going on.

The jib

Mark the jibsheet as a reference. It will hardly ever be lined up because there is an infinite range of sheet tensions needed. But it is very useful to be able to say something like 'Pull the sheet in until the mark is 2.5 cm (1 in.) from the fairlead'. I suggest you pull in the jibsheet hard, then let it off 5 cm (2 in.) and mark it at that point. Then take the sheets off, lay them parallel and mark the other one at exactly the same position so they are symmetrical.

Once you're sailing you will be constantly adjusting the jibsheet – in in a gust, out in a lull. But to begin with, cleat it to give the helm a chance to get 'in the groove'.

The jib fairlead is restricted by the class rules. Mount it on the thwart with a 25 mm riser.

The jib tack line needs a mark on the rope and a scale on the foredeck.

The mainsail

As with the jibsheet, put a mark on the mainsheet to act as a guide.

Put three marks on the *downhaul* (on other boats this is called the Cunningham). These are your approximate settings for light, medium and strong winds. Of course, when the downhaul is tight it opens up the top of the leech and depowers the sail.

The *clew outhaul* has two marks, one for beating and one for running. Reaching settings are in between. Make the upwind mark so there is a 10 cm (4 in.) gap between the foot of the sail and the boom, and the downwind mark so there is a 15 cm (6 in.) gap. Note that on a light wind run, the outhaul may be very tight.

The *kicking strap (vang)* is the main control on most boats and it's vital to know how much tension you have on it. Assuming you have a cascade system, make a mark on the fixed line and view a block moving past it.

The spinnaker

Mark the spinnaker sheet for close reaching. Set the pole just off the forestay and mark the guy where it enters the cleat. Repeat on the other side.

Put a mark on the jib luff to show a good pole height.

The daggerboard

With the boat on its trolley, carefully put in the daggerboard. The pads will hold it in the fully 'up' position – mark this on the board. Then take it out and put a mark at the halfway point.

Mast rake

To measure mast rake hoist the end of a tape measure to the top of the mast (see diagram opposite). Pull it tight down to the bottom black band (by the boom). Adjust the halyard until the top of the black band measures 13 ft 9 in. (4200 mm). This ensures you have the tape measure hoisted to the standard position. Now swing the tape measure aft and measure to the top of the centre of the transom 16 ft 9 in. (5100 mm) is a good starting rake.

Rig tension

You measure rig tension with the boat on the trolley and the sails down. Take your Loos gauge (or similar) and clip it onto a shroud at nose height. Pull the string and read the tension. About 15 is right as a general setting. Less in light winds and more in strong winds, though on a Mirror, without spreaders, trying to increase rig tension only bends the mast.

Note that the gauges all read slightly differently, so if you want to compare your rig to someone else's you need to use the same gauge on each.

Table of settings of vang, Cunningham etc for various wind strengths

	Kicker/ Vang	Downhaul	Outhaul mid-boom	Mast Rake	Rig Tension	Jib Halyard Tension	Jib Sheet Tension
Light Winds	Slack	None	a clenched fist between sail and boom	5100	12 on Loose	Very small sags between hanks	Light
Medium Wind	Take the slack out	Just a bit to remove some wrinkles	An open hand	5050	14	No sags between hanks	Medium
Strong Wind	on hard	Used to de-power leech when pulled hard	less than a fist	5000	16	No sags but no knuckle	Hard

Hull finish

There has been endless debate on whether a shiny finish or a matt finish is faster. In my view either will do but it's easier to keep a matt finish up to standard (you just have to run a piece of wet-and-dry over it) so I suggest you go for that.

Even more important is that there must be **absolutely no projections** to cause drag. Also note that the first third of the hull, rudder and centreboard are the crucial areas (after that, laminar flow is lost anyway) so, if time is tight, spend your time there.

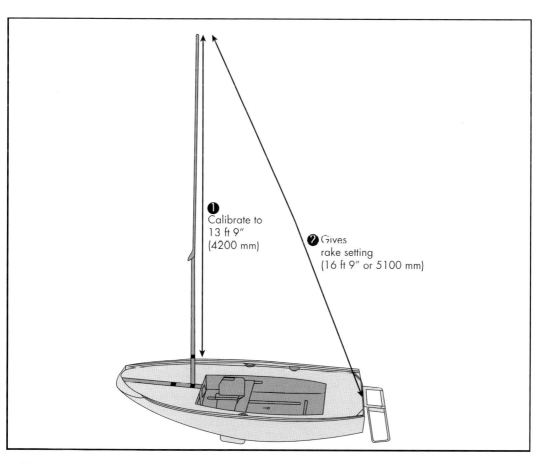

❶ Calibrate to 13 ft 9" (4200 mm)

❷ Gives rake setting (16 ft 9" or 5100 mm)

26.1

The front of the rudder blade is particularly important. Also, on a Mirror, there is a hole in the skeg. The new rules allow you to fill it, which is what I recommend.

Centre mainsheet

The centre mainsheet is definitely faster. When you fit one, move the bottom take-off point of the kicker to the bottom of the mast, to give the crew more room to move.

At the time of writing, the bridle arrangement (at the transom) is still not defined. But whatever system you fit, make sure that you can get the boom to lie along the centreline of the boat. This will mean adjusting the bridle until the blocks touch. But be careful not to put too much tension on the leech and remember you may have to sacrifice the central alignment slightly to keep the leech open.

In the centre of the boat, fit a good quality ratchet block, preferably without a cleat. This will encourage you to play the sheet all the time, something that is second nature to Laser sailors.

Note in passing that if you still have the original stern sheeting system you pull in the mainsheet until the leeward part of the yoke is vertical.

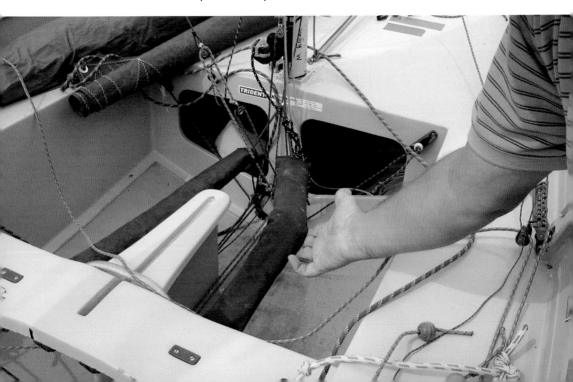

Yet more free speed

- Fit the Bermudian rig. It has less windage and more power. But be aware that there may be the odd wind strength where the gaff rig is still faster.

- Fit a 4:1 kicker, led aft to the thwart.

- Fit an adjustable toestrap, padded for comfort.

- Attach non-slip neoprene to the gunwales.

- Cut all ropes to the correct length.

- Fit self-bailers that work, and don't leak.

- Make sure your transom holes are max size, for flushing.

- All fittings must work and be sprayed daily with WD40 or MacLube silicon spray.

- Make sure that the rudder is vertical when down. On the original boat, the hole in the rudder blade was too far back, so the blade caught on the corner of the stock before the blade could get vertical. In this case you needed to fill the hole and drill another further forward. Then you can steer accurately and with feel.

- Put woollies on each shroud.

- Fit telltales to the jib. Three up the luff and one on the leech two-thirds of the way up.

- Fit telltales on the main. One on the leech at each batten pocket (see photo page 9), and two on the body of the sail one metre up from the tack and 45 cm (18 in.) and 60 cm (24 in.) back from the luff.

- Fit a compass on the foredeck, far enough forward that it doesn't catch the sheets and where both the crew and helm can see it.

Rope Sizes Chart

In summary, tuning is really a question of adjusting the mast rake and shroud tension and moving the jib up and down at the task. Simple really. Get that boat sorted, then go out and win!

Rope Sizes Chart

Rope	Suggested Colour	Type	Width	Length
Main sheet	Any		6mm	11 m
Jib Sheet	White Yellow easy to mark	Soft Taper the bit you don't hold	6mm	5 m
Spinnaker sheet	Bright easy to find	Tapered	4mm	12 m
Spinaker halyard/ downhaul	Any	Dynema	4 mm	15 m
Jib halyard	Any	Dynema	4 mm	8 m
Main Halyard	Any	Stripped Dynema	4 to 2 mm	8 m
Kicker / Vang	Grey	Stripped	3 mm	3 m
Kicker/Vang control	Red	Soft on the hands: the most used control	4 mm	6 m

27 BOATSPEED

Straight line boatspeed is boring – but without it you can't win races.

You can't get boatspeed on your own, and you can't get it racing because you only make sail adjustments then. Nobody is ever big enough to stop racing, make a change and rejoin the fray.

In the 60s the great Rodney Pattisson owned two Flying Dutchmen and sailed them alongside each other day in, day out in Poole Bay, painstakingly changing one thing at a time until he had worked out the best gear to use and the best settings. He won two gold medals and one silver medal in three Olympics.

The rest of us have to be content with the Buddy System or Squad Training.

Buddy System

Ideally you will choose the national champion as your buddy. However, you are likely to improve a lot more than he does, so realistically you will choose someone who goes the same speed as you.

Begin by tuning on a beat. Arrange the boats as in diagram 27.1, one boat slightly ahead and to leeward. You should be close enough to be in the same wind but not so close that the windward boat is backwinded (lee bowed).

Sail until you can see if one boat is faster. Stop and chat about why you think this is. Then change one thing on the slower boat and sail again. If it speeds up, leave the change. If not, revert to the original setting and change something else.

When the two boats are going the same speed, the (original) faster boat can make a change. If this helps, then the other boat also makes the change, and so on.

You may need to come ashore sometimes to change rake or make some other big alteration. So be it – this isn't a quick process! (But, as they say, 'Boatspeed makes you a tactical genius'.)

When you have fast settings, write them down and mark them on the boat and on the ropes.

Of course, you've only got boatspeed in the 'wind of the day'. You'll need sessions for strong, medium and light winds.

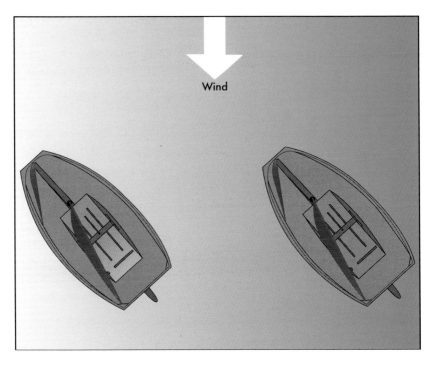

27.1 Buddy tuning to windward.

You should tune downwind also. Remember, you can typically grind past a couple of boats on a beat but you may be able to fly past 10 or more downwind.

Set up the boats alongside, and once again sail to establish who is faster. Then make a change **one thing at a time** until you find what speeds that boat up.

Occasionally you may find that you simply cannot bring one boat up to speed. More drastic measures may be needed, such as:

- New sails

- New foils

- New mast

- New boom

- Change of rake

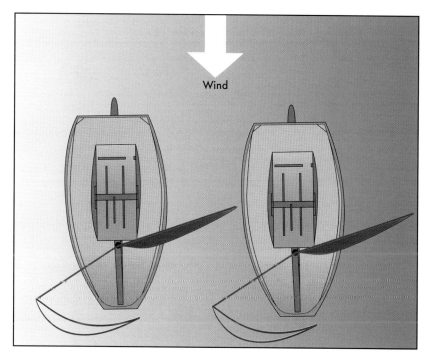

27.2 Buddy tuning downwind.

- Change of jib tack position
- Change of jib fairlead position
- New hull

The squad system

If you are lucky enough to be in a squad, your coach will help you develop speed. He may use the offset triangle for training. Here you sail a series of one-sided beats, with a triangle returning the boats to the start, keeping them out of the way of the stragglers (Figure 27.3). The coach will suggest a change and you can test it out on the next little beat. You also get plenty of starting practice.

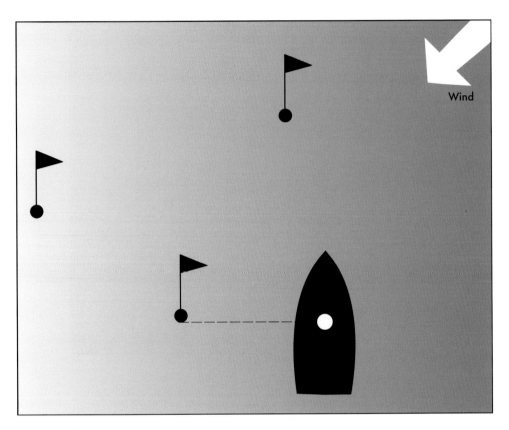

27.3 An offset triangle.

28 ADVANCED BOAT HANDLING

Draw a dartboard and make a segment for each boat handling technique you think is important. Mine are:

1. Starting

2. Trim

3. Tacking

4. Rounding the windward mark

5. Gybing

6. Spinnaker drop

7. Planing

8. Penalty turns.

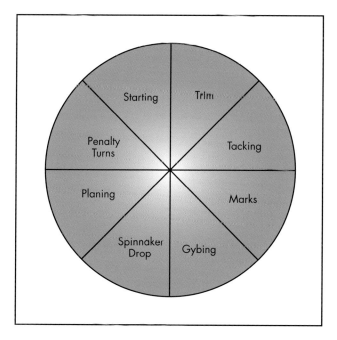

28.1 Advanced boat handling.

Score yourself out of 10 for each, where 10 is perfection! Then work on your weakest skills.

1 Starting

If you win the start, you are well on the way to winning the race.

The skills you need for a good start are:

- Good timing
- Good position
- Good acceleration
- Ability to slow
- Ability to stop
- Ability to hover
- Ability to slip sideways
- Ability to get out of irons.

Timing

The crew is responsible for counting down to the start. Agree how often the crew will call, for example, every 15 seconds from 5 minutes to 3 minutes, then every 10 seconds, then every 5 seconds from one minute. The crew can encourage the helm to push forward by counting more frequently!

Good position

You should agree your starting plan well before the five-minute gun, and also how you plan to get into this position. 'We'll start two-thirds of the way down the line because there is a 5° bias to the pin end, but I don't want to be in the pile up near the pin. We'll reach along the line on port and tack at one minute to go in our chosen spot'. Get a transit before the warning signal, making sure it's fixed (a cow might move!).

When you tack into position, make sure you turn onto a close-hauled course so you acquire luffing rights. (It's no good turning halfway and staying head to wind, for example. Under the rules, you are still tacking and have few rights.) Note you don't have to pull in your sails, just turn onto the close-hauled course.

Choose your neighbours carefully when you tack. Ideally you will finish up a boat length to windward of a rabbit. Try not to line up beside the world champion. Note that you must line up on somebody. If you just tack and leave a huge gap below you, someone else will come in underneath you and ruin your start.

You now have a minute to go and will be wriggling like mad to make and keep a gap to leeward. The helm is squeezing up and calling the boat to windward to keep clear. Your crew is looking all around to warn of hunters coming into your gap. As they approach, tell them there's no room, and turn the bow downwind while pushing out the boom. The boat is immediately four feet wider! But don't go backwards. Use your skill to stay on station without going forwards.

Ability to slow

In the pre-start line-up you have to be able to slow down. You can let out the sails until they flap (photo 1), luff up to head to wind, or heel the boat to leeward but bear away at the same time. Or you can use a combination of these.

Ability to stop

The best method is to push the boom out hard (photo 2). Indeed, in the pre-start the crew should always be pushing out the boom. If the helm wants to stop, he lets out the

mainsheet. If he wants to go, pulling in the mainsheet will easily overcome the crew's pushing.

Ability to hover

Let the jib flap, but control the sheet so it's only just slack (you don't want to have miles of sheet to pull in when you're trying to accelerate).

Then adjust the mainsheet against the crew's push on the boom (photos 2 and 3).

Ability to slip sideways

Raise the daggerboard if you need to slide sideways without going forwards.

Ability to get out of irons

If the boat stops head to wind let out the mainsheet and let off the kicking strap(vang). These actions will open the leech of the main. Then back the jib. You will now be going backwards so push the tiller away to turn the bow downwind (photos 4 and 5). Next, release the windward jibsheet and pull in the leeward jibsheet. Finally, pull in a little mainsheet.

Good acceleration

You will have worked out how long it takes to get to full speed from a standing start.

Say this is seven seconds. Assuming you're just behind the line, with seven seconds to go you must accelerate, even if those around you don't. But if the black flag is flying, move forward with the line of boats.

Heel the boat to leeward with the sheets out slightly. Now 'pull the trigger'. Bring the boat upright, sheeting in at the same time. Be careful not to break Rule 42.

The first 50m(165ft) are the most important of the race. Sail flat out, with 110% effort. Work the mainsheet. Hike like crazy. Squeeze to windward whenever possible, then foot to regain speed. You're trying to maintain your lane, and keep up on the boat to leeward.

It's vital to practise starting. Here are five exercises that will help:

1 Pack of cards

Each boat in the squad is designated a card: Ace, 2, 3, 4, 5, 6, 7, 8, 9, 10 and the rest are Jokers.

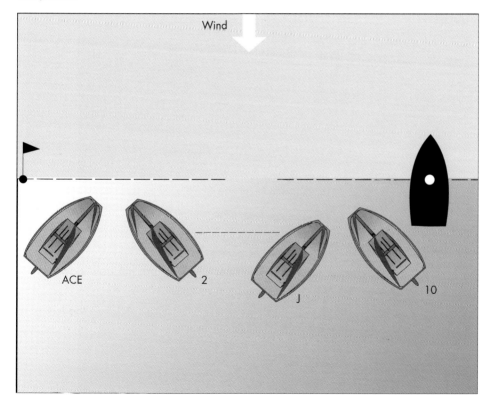

28.2 Pack of cards.

We have a 3, 2, 1 countdown and then the 10 boats have to start in the position of their card, Ace trying a port tack start by the pin, then 2 on starboard next to him, 3 on starboard next along, and so on until 10 is starting on starboard by the committee boat. The Jokers try to sneak into the gaps in the line-up and spoil the others' starts.

I am amazed how well people start with these quite severe constraints.

2 Time and distance
Set up a short line with two boat lengths between the ends. Ideally there are five boats in the exercise. Give a one minute 'gun' and start at zero. Repeat several times.

3 Hovering
You need one mark per boat. Sail up to your mark, stop and try to stay in the same position for 90 seconds.

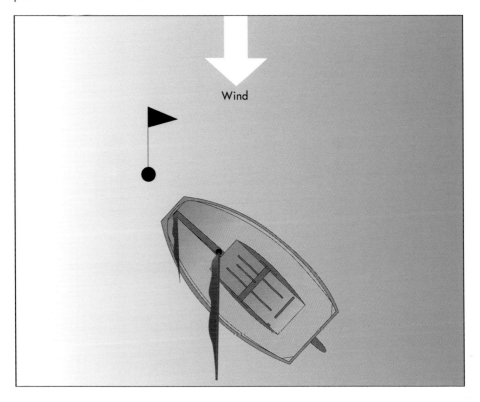

Wind

28.3 Hovering.

4 Double tack

Use your mark again. This time, come in below the lay line to the mark and stop. Then make two tacks to take your bow to the mark, but without going forwards. Use the crew's hand on the boom to control your speed. If you have a look at the CD in Ben Ainslie's book *The Laser Campaign Manual* you will see how dynamic top sailors are at the start.

In addition to moving the boat to windward, a double tack is also a good way of burning time if you are early.

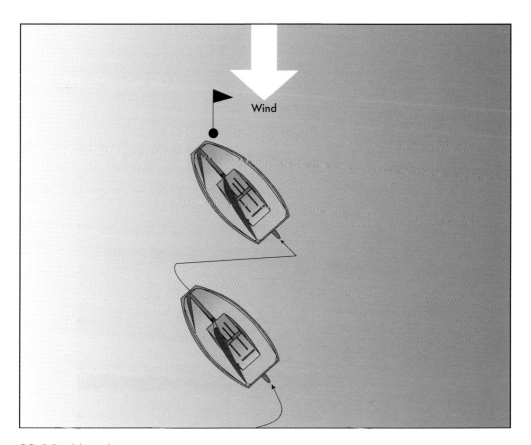

28.4 Double tack.

5 Lots of little races

The clock runs continuously and there is a three-minute countdown. Start, sail for one minute then get back quickly for the next start (in effect you will have one minute to manoeuvre when you have got back). Every third start is a 'go', in other words you race to the windward mark and back.

2 Trim

Trim fore-and-aft and sideways is important.

Upwind the transom should just kiss the water, with the bow just out. The boat should be dead upright except in very light winds when you can let her heel to get the sails to fall into shape and reduce wetted area.

Downwind kite the boat to windward. This raises the main into faster air and gives neutral helm. Unfortunately the kite moves into slower air, but this can't be helped and the mainsail is bigger.

3 Tacking

Make sure that the crew can get between the kicker and the mainsheet. It helps if the kicker is attached to the foot of the mast instead of the floor. In light winds consider taking

28.5 Maximise the space between the kicker and the mainsheet.

the kicker off altogether or moving the boom attachment forward. Rake the mainsheet a little to increase the space.

Your objective is initially to heel the boat to leeward so it turns up into the wind. Keep the power on as long as possible by pulling in the mainsheet as you turn. Once through the eye of the wind, roll the boat on top of you and let the mainsheet out a bit. Finally, roll the boat upright while pulling in the mainsheet again.

A common mistake is to roll the boat upright too early. You need it heeled to help the boat turn.

Some helms like the jib to back briefly, others don't. Both seem to work equally well.

The crew tacks facing aft, which means the front foot goes across first. Punch your sheet hand into the air to pull the jibsheet in fast.

The helm lets the boat heel to leeward, then initiates the tack with trigger words like 'Let's go!' Note the tiller should go no further than the middle of the side buoyancy tank, or you will really put on the brakes.

Here are four exercises to sharpen you up.

1. Tacking on the whistle.

2. Tack, then steer with the tiller behind your back for 10 seconds (photo 6). There is no need to change hands immediately.

3. Tack in slow motion. People always try to tack too quickly.

4. You will often scoop water over the side when you roll tack. Practise leaning back so the water runs out of the holes above the stern deck, rather than into the bottom of the boat. I call this flushing.

4 Rounding the windward mark

There are two ways to approach the mark. Generally you will make a low approach on starboard, tacking across towards the lay line 20 metres or so from the buoy, then tacking back onto starboard on the lay line or just above it. Alternatively, approach on port if you are certain you can find a gap. Mirrors are notorious for overstanding, so you may well be able to tack below the line of starboard boats. Of course, you have no rights as you come in on port, and beware Rule 18.3 'Tacking at a Mark'.

Assuming you are rounding onto a reach, decide well beforehand if you are initially going to go high or low. Approaching the mark on starboard, keep sailing hard until you are certain you will lay the buoy. Only then start adjusting things – let the downhaul off completely (but re-cleat the rope), set the outhaul for the reach and let off the kicker to the reaching marks. Wait until you are level with the mark before you start to launch the spinnaker pole (if you put it up earlier some idiot may come in on port and crash into you, or you may not lay the mark, and with the pole up you can't tack). Now, in a blur of speed, hoist, put the guy into the cleat, have the helm set the kite while steering with the tiller between his legs, and pull up the daggerboard to the reaching position.

If you are rounding onto the run, decide well before the buoy whether you are going to do a bear-away set or a gybe set. For the latter, leave the pole down until after the gybe, but hoist the kite immediately – you can fill it without the pole and make a gain while the pole is going out.

5 Gybing

Gybe when the boat is going fast: the pressure in the sail (the apparent wind) is lowest then. The crew can assist by:

- Helping the spinnaker pole go back along the boom.

- Pulling the old guy so the kite is behind the mainsail after the gybe.

- Pulling the boom across.

The helm can also help pull the boom across, but his main job is to steer accurately. The commonest problem is broaching onto a reach after the gybe, so be sure to reverse the tiller just after the boom comes over, that is, sail an S-shaped course.

To practise gybing we get everyone following-my-leader in line on a reach. The coach gives two whistles and everyone bears away onto a run and hoists the spinnaker. Then they gybe on each whistle. Finally the coach gives two whistles to tell everyone to drop. This exercise hedges the boats in, so is more realistic than simply doing gybes in open water.

Note that on a well set up boat the sheets have knots to prevent their going out too far.

6 Spinnaker drop

Make sure you drop early enough to have everything stowed before you begin the turn. It is better to drop too early than too late.

The worst thing is to go below the leeward mark. If you go a boat length below it, for example, you will lose more than two boat lengths.

We practise roundings by putting out a hand to touch the mark. Remember: wide in, tight out, so you are in a high lane have the option to tack if you want to.

7 Planing

You are allowed to pump on each wave to get on the plane (photos 7 and 8). Pump the spinnaker guy and   sheet and the mainsheet together and also use your weight.

If there is much wind the crew can move aft and share the helm's toestrap.

Work hard to sail downhill all the time and move your body weight to keep on the plane.

8 Penalty turns

A Two-Turns Penalty consists of two tacks and two gybes.

Whether you begin with a tack or gybe is up to you, and depends on which gives clearer water to turn in.

On a beat use lots of heel so you don't use the rudder more then 45°. Heel to leeward to luff and to windward to bear away. Sail the boat round.

Offwind you will need to take down the kite before you begin.

Here are some exercises to help:

- On the whistle everyone does a Two-Turns Penalty. The winner is the boat that finishes first.

- Alternatively, just time the turns.

You must take your penalties in races so practise them. And don't forget to sign the Turns Sheet when you come ashore.

29 ADVANCED CREWING

As you gain in confidence as a crew, you will take responsibility for more areas. You will:

- Move about the boat freely, working her through waves and rolling her on tacks and gybes.

- Be given control of timing at the start and the distance to go to the line. This frees the helm to concentrate on the boats around.

- Adjust the jib without instructions, letting out the sheet when the wind drops and hardening it when a gust arrives.

- Feed the helm with relevant tactical info: 'John has tacked, maybe we should go'.

- Know where all the opposition are at all times.

- Call gusts and watch for lifts and headers.

- Be part of the tactical team, calling the laylines and deciding whether to tack or duck starboard boats.

- Point out the next mark.

- Remind the helm about tides, especially near marks.

- Help with the decision on whether it's to be a bear-away set or a gybe set.

- Organise the spinnaker pole and guy as you approach the windward mark.

- Make sure the spinnaker never flaps once it's up. Report on the pressure in the kite so the helm can sail lower in higher pressure.

- Trim the daggerboard.

- Make sure that nearby boats are obeying the rules, particularly if this is in your favour.

- Push down the daggerboard before gybing and pull it up afterwards.

- Balance the boat while gybing. The main job is to keep the red bits (the sails) out of the blue bits (the water)!

- Time the spinnaker drop so everything is tidied away as you exit the leeward mark. If in doubt, drop the kite earlier, particularly if there are tactical reasons – the only place to be is right by the buoy and you may need to slow down to achieve this.

- On the last leg, help decide if you're going to attack the boat in front (high risk strategy) or cover the boats behind (low risk).

- Assess which end of the finish line looks the closest.

So, you can see that crewing is no easy option and is vital to the boat's success!

30 RACE PREPARATION

'If you fail to prepare, be prepared to fail'.

There are a lot of things in sailing that we can't be sure about. But anything we can be sure about, we should know.

This is best achieved by devising a routine for yourself, and following it every time you're going to a regatta. A good routine calms the nerves, as well as giving information.

At home

Check the weather on the web. Begin three days before the regatta, but take these early forecasts with a pinch of salt. Obviously, the day before you can take the prediction a bit more seriously. Try www.windguru.cz and www.xcweather.co.uk and www.bbc.co.uk/weather. Also try the local sailing club, which may have a weather link.

Tides are much more predictable. www.bbc.co.uk/weather has tide tables, as do almanacs.

Check the lie of the land on Google Earth. Play around with various wind directions, trying to predict what would happen at the venue. You will need to refer to *Wind Strategy* by David Houghton and Fiona Campbell for effects like convergence, divergence, shifts and the sea breeze.

Download the sailing instructions and laminate them ready to take afloat.

Note the start time and work back to find the time you should leave home. You need to arrive at least 1 hour 30 minutes before the start and be afloat at least three-quarters of an hour before.

When you arrive at the venue

Have a look at the weather, particularly the clouds. Usually, clouds mean wind. Are the clouds going the same way as the surface wind?

Look for patches of wind and calm areas on the racecourse. Remember, everything David Houghton says sometimes happens.

If you arrive at low tide, check where the shallow patches are ('the geography' as i call it).

Talk to the locals and ask things like 'when does the tide change?' It never changes exactly at high water.

Going out to the start

As you sail out, come onto the wind occasionally and take compass readings on port and starboard tack. Write them down and look for a pattern. Is the wind bending, progressively, shifting one way, or oscillating? What is the mean heading on each tack?

Sail past a mark and check for tide or current. Note that on big lakes there is sometimes a current, particularly when the wind has been blowing in one direction for several days, then reverses.

Stand up in the boat and check the lie of the land to windward. Valleys and hills give predictable shifts. Try to work out the causes of any effects you've seen.

Make a plan

Think about what you've seen and discovered. What would you now expect to pay on the racecourse? If you have two opposing effects, which would you expect to win?

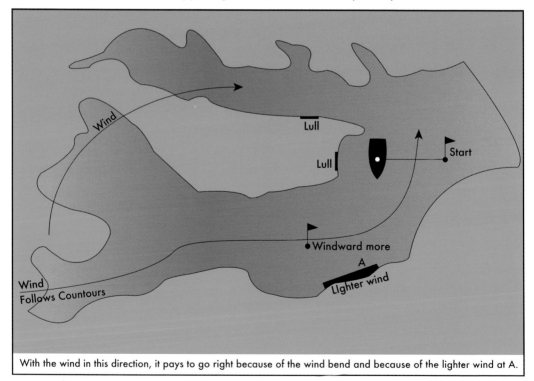

With the wind in this direction, it pays to go right because of the wind bend and because of the lighter wind at A.

30.1

If, for example, the indications are you should go right, don't just blast out to the lay line in one go. Wiggle your way across, taking advantage of small shifts. Remember, you are aiming for a top ten place at the windward mark, not a glorious first (or last!).

What is the weather forecast? Will the wind continue, so that your plan holds for race two as well? Remember: it does what it does when it's doing it!

Don't forget to plan for the downwind legs too – remember, you can take far more boats downwind than upwind.

Test the plan

If you have time, sail upwind from the start line to confirm your predictions. This is even better if you can split tacks with your buddy, sailing for two minutes then tacking back and watching who is ahead. Tim Davison recounted how, in a Laser nationals, he and his buddy split tacks for five minutes from the upcoming start near Drake's Island in Plymouth Sound. When they tacked back, the buddy had disappeared! Eventually, a small dot appeared on the horizon, running back towards him. The buddy had gained nearly a mile in ten minutes by going right! Armed with this knowledge, both started last through the gate and got to the windward mark first and second in a fleet of over 100 boats, despite one of them capsizing en route. The buddy system works!

31 TRAVELLING TO AN EVENT

The golden rule is to keep everything together as one unit. That way, all you have to do is hitch the boat onto the back of the car, and go. But if you've taken something out and put it in the garage, for example, you'll probably forget it!

If you do have to remove something, stick a note onto the trailer to remind you.

The photo shows a good tie-down arrangement, with the gaff, boom and spinnaker pole secured to two bars.

Trailer

Choose a trailer that fits the boat. Test it to make sure it's roadworthy, and carry a suitable jack and spare wheel. The wheel nuts may be a different size from those on the car, so carry a suitable spanner. A foot pump completes the ensemble. Towing RIBs as much as I do, I've found that big wheels are much better than small ones – they turn fewer times per journey.

Choose the chocks with the biggest area to spread the load on the hull. Always use a bottom cover, especially after all your hard work polishing the hull!

Trailer board

In my experience trailer boards fail all too often. It's a shame someone doesn't make a better, more expensive one. Carry a spare bulb for each bulb type (this is compulsory on the Continent).

Speed limits

At home you can trail at 30mph in built-up areas, 50mph on an unrestricted single carriageway and 60mph on a dual carriageway or motorway. Remember: you aren't allowed in the third (fast) lane of a three-lane motorway. If you're going abroad check the speed limits.

The car

A bit of planning will make sure you arrive at the regatta in good shape. Alistair MacKenzie, for example, has a king-sized camper van and drives it to regattas with Anna and Holly in the back. The girls can do their homework, watch TV and sleep while he takes the strain. They might leave Windermere at 5pm on a Friday and arrive in Weymouth at 2am on Saturday, but the girls are expending no effort and don't need to wake up until 8am. With this sort of back-up it's not surprising they are World Champions (but Dr MacKenzie does sometimes take an afternoon nap!).

In any case it's a good idea to take a DVD or iPod in the car – the last thing you want on your way to a regatta is an argument about which radio station should be playing. You also want to prevent boredom.

Timing the journey

The Notice of Race (NOR) will give you the start time of the first race. Obviously, you work back from there to decide when to leave.

In many ways the race starts when you leave home! Try to keep the stress level down by:

- Looking up the host club on the Internet.

- Working out your route.

- Filling the tank the night before. (A stop may set you back 20 minutes.) While you're at it, fill the windscreen washer bottle, check the oil and pump up the tyres on the car and trailer.

To win it you've got to be in it. At the very least that means arriving on time.

32 STRATEGY

Strategy is loosely defined as where you would go if there was no-one else on the racecourse. (Tactics is how you manoeuvre against other boats.)

But note that, however good your plan, you must be adaptable. Things go wrong, and you will have to modify your strategy accordingly. Indeed, **sailing is all about coping with adversity**. Few sports have so many variables and so many opportunities for mistakes. We are even powered by something we can't see!

The start

We have made a plan and our heart rate is rising as the start is looming.

1. The first thing to do is get a transit. Assuming you want to start mid-line, take your transit from a position two lengths to leeward of the starboard end of the line (32.1). Then, when you are using your transit to position the boat

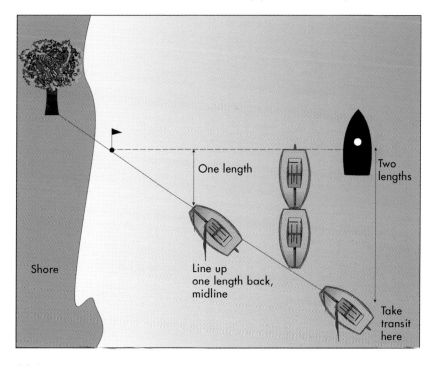

32.1 Getting a transit.

just before the gun, you will automatically be one boat length back. That allows you to sheet in with 7 seconds to go and hit the line with full speed.

2. Next, sail up and down the line to check which is the favoured end. The 'hardest' end to get to is the one where you want to start (32.2).

3. You can also go head to wind and take a bearing with your compass, then sail down the line and take another bearing. If the difference is less than 90°, you are heading for the favoured end of the line. Personally, I prefer the first method.

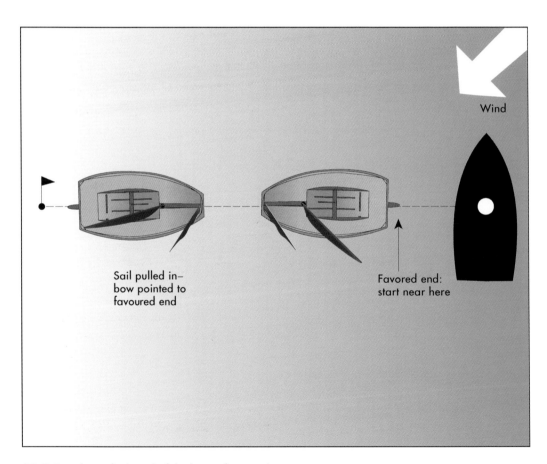

Wind

Sail pulled in—
bow pointed to
favoured end

Favored end:
start near here

32.2 Deciding which end of the line is favoured.

4. Now check the way the boat drifts at slow speed. Sail close to a buoy and hover. Learn how your boat behaves – how fast it drifts sideways and backwards. This will be worse in strong winds and big waves. With a port-biased line you may drift down so far that you can't lay the pin!

The Mirror has a lot of sideways drift and, perhaps because of this, the fleet is notorious for mid-line sag. By keeping drift to a minimum and keeping moving forward you can make a great start here.

The crew counts down, gradually reducing the period like this: 5, 4.30, 4 . . . 60, 50, 40 . . . 10, 9, 8 . . . 3, 2, 1, go! Of course, if the crew reckons the boat is too far back, they give the time more often. (A small hint: set your watch to count down from five minutes, but let it run for two seconds and stop it. Then, when the five-minute gun goes, count to yourself 5, 4.59, 4. 58 while fumbling for the button and start the watch on 4.58. If you leave your watch set on 5 minutes, by the time you have rolled back your sleeve and found the button you are bound to push it late, which will confuse you at the start.)

Exercises for starting

1. **RIB start.** When there is no wind – or too much – practise starting in a RIB. You are allowed to take a transit, but not to drive down the line. You get a three-minute signal and are marked out of ten on how close to the line you are when the gun goes.

2. **Long line.** The coach sets up a long line with the windward mark only 25m (82ft) from it. This is a fleet start, but there is really only one place to start – on the lay line to the buoy (32.3). This is very good practice for lining up pre-start.

3. **Box start.** The coach sets up a trapezoidal 'box' from four buoys. You must not go outside the box in the last two minutes before the start (32.4).

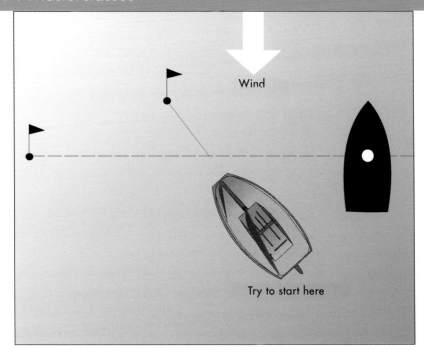

32.3 A starting exercise.

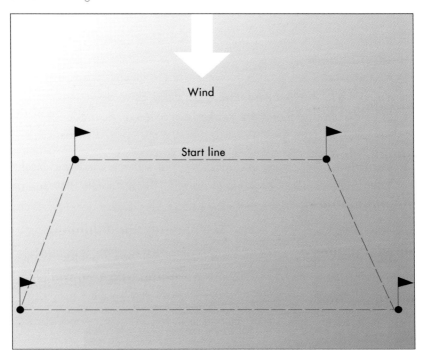

32.4 Manoeuvring 'in the box'.

After the start

A good way of looking at the beat is shown in 32.5.

You can describe your route by the numbers, for example 1, 2, 5, 8, 9. You would have to have a very good reason to include a 4 or a 6!

Note that sector 9 is also divided because your course here is critical. If you are in the top five approaching the mark, aim for an imaginary buoy at mini-position 5. If you are on starboard and the wind lifts, you will probably make the real buoy. If it heads, you can tack and again reap the reward. But, of course, don't try this if you are further down the fleet. Then you have to keep right and join the queue. Balance risk with reward.

Back to the race. If you are going well after the start, stay with your group and race them. Your objective is to win your side of the beat: obviously, you can't do anything about the boats on the other side. BUT if you see them benefiting from a shift, be ready to cut your losses and get across to their side.

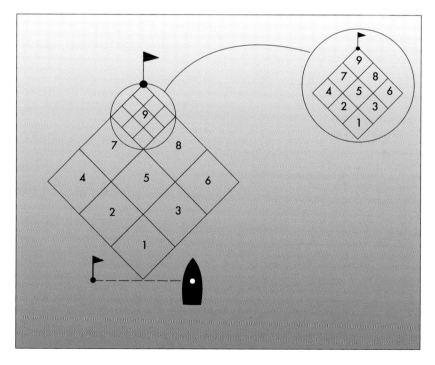

32.5 How to describe your route up the beat.

If there isn't a windshift in the first two minutes, tack anyway to get back to the centre of the course.

If you are doing well, balance risk with reward and sail the fleet. In 32.6 you are A. If the three boats ahead go left and the pack behind goes right, the low risk strategy is to go right. That way, you attack the leaders and defend against the rest. The lowest you should come is fourth and you could win!

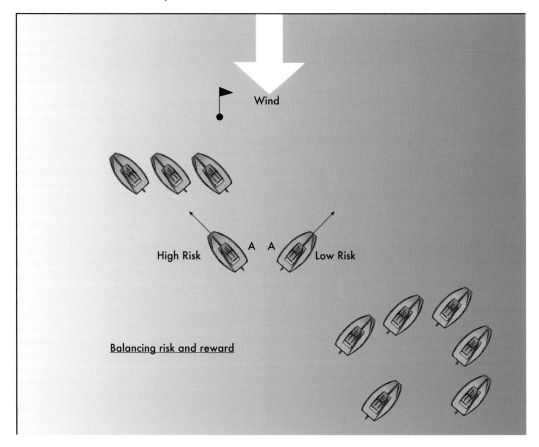

32.6 Balance risk and reward.

On the reach

Take a transit as you go round the windward mark. As you sail down the reach your aim is to keep the background still behind the wing mark.

Work out whether to go high or low:

- If the tide is pushing you up, definitely go low.

- If the wind is very strong, consider going high, then setting the kite later.

- If there are a lot of boats behind, go high. If there are a lot of boats in front (and few behind) go low. Try to plane down the leeward stern wave of the boat in front.

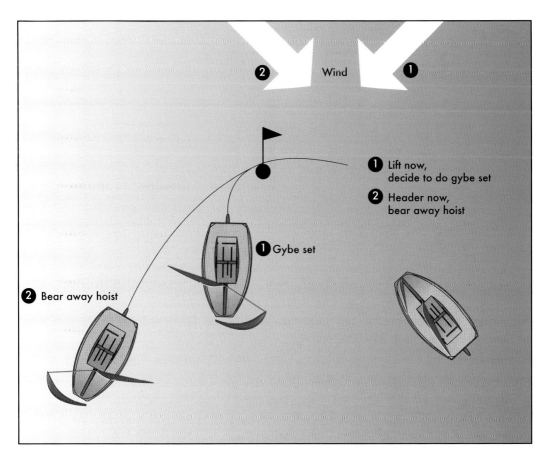

32.7 Deciding which gybe you will take on the run.

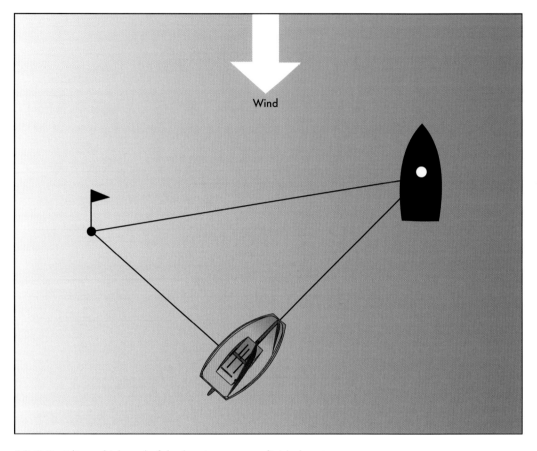

Wind

32.8 Deciding which end of the line is nearest – finish there!

On the run

Before you get to the leeward mark, discuss which side of the beat is better from the point of view of wind pressure and tide.

As you approach the mark, if you are on a lift then plan to do a gybe set. If you are on a header, simply hoist the spinnaker as you go round the mark.

If there are a lot of boats around you may have to modify your plan. For example, if a bunch of boats follow you round, then defend by gybing away to find clear air. If you round behind a bunch, attack by trying to blanket them.

Use your burgee to spot shifts on the run. Keep the pressure on but sail as low as possible, maximising your VMG (Velocity Made Good).

Remember, your roles are reversed on the run compared with the beat: the crew concentrates on the spinnaker while the helm looks around for wind and thinks about tactics and strategy.

The finish

Operate risk management on the last beat. If there are three boats ahead and one behind, attack. If there's one ahead and three behind, defend. If the boats behind are going the way you want them to, apply loose cover. Otherwise cover them tightly until they tack and go the way you want.

As you get close to the finish sail towards on end. As you cross the layline to the other end, assess which is nearer and aim to finish there.

Remember: it's not over 'til the fat lady hoots!

33 PARENTS, COACHES, BE YOUR OWN COACH

In this final section I am going to look at people who can help.

Parents

Parents are an asset! They provide, transport, food, the boat and technical back-up.

I like to involve parents, not least because – if I send them away – I lose control of them! In any case, they'll be in the car with the sailors on the way home, so it's better if they understand what's been going on. I try to have a parents, meeting at some point in every training weekend, with an opportunity for questions.

It's important that parents understand what a coach does. Coaching is not teaching – for example, if things are going well, the coach says nothing! A good coach will set up an exercise, then stand back and watch while the sailor does the learning. Sailing is different from football, where the coach is in control during the event. In our sport the coach isn't even allowed on the racecourse, so we have to lead the sailors towards being able to do everything themselves.

In the same way, parents should gradually let the kids do everything for themselves. In three or four years time the child will be driving him or herself to events, so don't wait until the day before their 17th birthday to withdraw from rigging, stocking up on food and so on.

In the early stages it's very helpful if parents stick to a good onshore routine, looking after nutrition, hydration, sun protection and sleep. They should aim to cover the 'duty of care' for their children.

On the water, observe but give no input. Let the coaches coach. After the race give (realistic) praise. But if your child has done badly, leave the post-mortem until later. After a cooling-off period the sailors will want to talk about what happened, and will probably come up with their own solutions to what went wrong.

Don't push too hard on the training front. For under 16s, weight training is out, and also back off during growth spurts.

If you would like to help still more, how about help running the Class Association?

Coaches

A good coach is

- Supportive

- Patient

- Professional

- Flexible

- Communicative

- Positive, regardless of the sailors' position in the race

- Committed to the sailor

- Proactive

- In harmony with the sailor.

If the sailor is in my squad, I prefer them not to have a private coach, or things can get confusing. But the child hasn't made the squad it is up to you whether or not to employ a coach.

Remember, coaches ask, teachers tell. If both were in the RIB, driving behind a Mirror with the kicker too tight, the teacher might say 'Let off the kicker!' while the coach might ask 'How's the mainsail leech looking?' The aim is always to get the sailors to learn for themselves.

Being your own coach

The best kind of self-coaching is to spend lots of time on the water, having fun with the boat. This improves boat handling. Play tennis-ball tag with your friends. (Throw the ball into the water. Try to pick it up before anyone else does, then throw it at another boat's

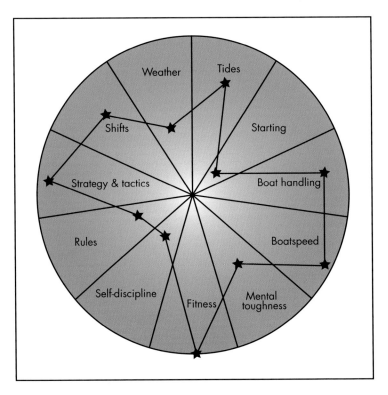

33.1 Important aspects of racing.

mainsail to score one point.) Practise going round marks. Then do ten tacks and three gybes. Deliberately capsize and right the boat as quickly as you can. Time yourself doing 720s. Up the anti as you get better.

Off the water, get fit (don't do weights if you are under 16). Spend time doing your own maintenance so that, when things break at a regatta, you can put the boat back together again.

As you improve, you may need a spot of self-analysis. Your objective is to control the controllables, and forget anything outside your control. Professionals use a dartboard diagram to help.

Make a list of things you think are important for racing. Among these might be:

- Starting

- Boat handling – tacking, gybing, rounding marks

- Boatspeed

- Mental toughness

- Fitness

- Self-discipline

- Rules knowledge

- Strategy and tactics

- Shifts

- Weather

- Tides.

Next, rate yourself out of 10 for each one: 10 is the level of the National Champion.

Fill in the dartboard, with one skill in each segment. Put a cross in the segment near the middle if your score is low, but near the perimeter if your score is high. You now have a picture of your current sailing skill

The plan is now to work on the areas where you are weakest.

For each training session decide what the objective is and how achieving this might help your performance. Then:

- Plan the activity

- Do it

- Review it.

PLAN – DO – REVIEW.

The buddy system is also a very powerful way of improving, and is the only way of increasing your boatspeed in practice.

Now you have speed, you'll have much more fun. Good luck, and see you on the racecourse!

Lifeboats

'Flat calm or force 10. I always wear one.'

Whether they're training or out on a shout, RNLI crew members always wear lifejackets. It's a rule informed by years of experience. They know that, whatever the weather, the sea's extremely unpredictable – and can turn at a moment's notice. They see people caught out all the time. People who've risked, or even lost their lives as a result. The fact is, a lifejacket will buy you vital time in the water – and could even save your life. But only if you're wearing it.

For advice on choosing a lifejacket and how to wear it correctly, call us on 0800 328 0600 (UK) or 1800 789 589 (RoI) or visit our website rnli.org.uk/seasafety/lifejackets

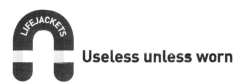

Useless unless worn

'Flat calm or force 10. I always wear one.'

Whether they're training or out on a shout, RNLI crew members always wear lifejackets. It's a rule informed by years of experience. They know that, whatever the weather, the sea's extremely unpredictable – and can turn at a moment's notice. They see people caught out all the time. People who've risked, or even lost their lives as a result. The fact is, a lifejacket will buy you vital time in the water – and could even save your life. But only if you're wearing it.

For advice on choosing a lifejacket and how to wear it correctly, call us on 0800 328 0600 (UK) or 1800 789 589 (RoI) or visit our website rnli.org.uk/seasafety/lifejackets

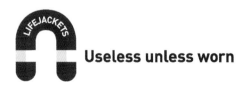

Useless unless worn